TORQUATO TASSO

JOHANN WOLFGANG von GOETHE

TORQUATO TASSO

A Play

Translated by
CHARLES E. PASSAGE
Associate Professor of Comparative Literature
Brooklyn College of The City University of New York

FREDERICK UNGAR PUBLISHING CO.
NEW YORK

INTRODUCTION

Slowly, at intervals through a ten-year period, Goethe worked out his five-act blank-verse *Torquato Tasso. A Drama* (Ein Schauspiel), publishing it at age forty-one, in 1790. Like *Iphigenia in Tauris*, its companion piece from the "Classical" decade of his life, the 1780's, it is "chamber music," so far removed from the manner of *Götz von Berlichingen* as to seem the work of another man. That "Storm and Stress" play of 1773, our author's first major literary success, is comparable to music for a large ensemble, with stirring tunes for horns and trumpets. By the same token those youthful prose plays of Schiller in the 1780's — *The Robbers, Fiesko,* and *Intrigue and Love* — are strident brass-band pieces, understandably repugnant to Goethe who had now come to feel that true art spoke with restraint, intensely but softly. In the perspectives of literary history this "chamber music" of *Tasso* looks backward to Racine, especially to *Bérénice,* and forward to the Turgenev of *A Month in the Country* and to the Chekhov of *The Cherry Orchard,* but it is, in itself, a unique production of a third kind within its tradition.

As the curtain rises on Act I a charming scene is revealed to the audience. Sunlight of an Italian springtime is bright amid a nook of formal Renaissance garden where two princesses, both mature women but not yet middle-aged, are conversing as old friends while their hands are occupied with the twining of garlands. Let us not insist that their casual attire be too strict a copy of feminine costume at the court of the Dukes of Ferrara around 1577, when the action is supposed to take place, because the author intended no historical reconstruction of a by-gone era. On the other hand let us not make either their costumes or the garden, anachronistically, too dreamily soft with Watteau's muted golds and greys.

Still less should these ladies be like those young persons, bright as butterflies, whom Fragonard would set to jesting with Eros beneath a vastness of trees and billowing clouds. In *this* garden there lurks an invisible spirit of relentless reality, and here, not many hours hence, utter catastrophe will plunge a gifted youth into despair and living death.

The invisible reality will not manifest itself as brutal violence or as wretched disease, nor will the hero be the innocent victim of captious authority or insidious court intrigue. These ladies are genuinely kindly; they cherish the youth in benevolent friendship; yet each will contribute to his spiritual destruction. The reigning Duke, who will presently step into this garden, is no tyrant; he is most graciously disposed toward the youth; yet he will do his part to effect the young man's ruin. The arriving visitor, Antonio Montecatino, last of the play's five characters to meet our eyes, is a generous, decent, upright man and a friend to all; yet he will be the one to initiate the process of the young man's downfall.

These four persons who destroy young Tasso are good human beings. All are mature, all are aware of his immaturity and willing and eager to make allowances for it. They are all wealthy persons, learned, worldly-wise, and socially gracious. Each has, in his own way, faced reality and effectively met its challenge — Alfonso II, Duke of Ferrara, as an able ruler concerned with all aspects of the welfare of his state and people; Antonio as an astute Secretary of State; Countess Leonore Sanvitale as wife and mother and lady of rank; Princess Leonore d'Este, the sister of Duke Alfonso, as a woman who has emerged from years of illness beneath the threat of imminent death to assume a role of earnest helpfulness to her brother and to all her friends. Yet each one of these four has a certain defect of character from which Tasso will suffer. It cannot have been by chance that the author conceived of these defects as qualities which are normally considered good but which, in this instance, are not so much exaggerated into faults as unfortunately juxtaposed, both to each other and to their victim. The very time and place are likewise to be deemed, normally, ideal, but in this instance disastrous for Tasso: it is the fairest spring weather and

the characters are enjoying a brief vacation in a rural pleasure
palace, far from city and court and routine duties. The fact that
all five friends have none but each other's company is accessory to
the hero's downfall.

The Duke, his Princess sister, and their guest the Countess
Leonore have had Tasso in their midst for some time. They know
him well. They are fond of him. Yet each entertains a misconcep-
tion of him, or at least a conception of him which *he* will find
intolerable.

For the Duke, Tasso is his court poet, whom it is an honor, a
privilege, and an obligation to support. He supports him gladly
and admits him to his most intimate circle. Only, he devoutly
wishes Tasso would bring to completion the great poem of
Jerusalem Delivered (Gerusalemme Liberata) over which such an
irksomely long time has been spent; and when Tasso seeks to go
away and take his manuscript with him, Alfonso is genuinely dis-
tressed to think some other prince will be the recipient of the
work which was to have redounded to the glory of the court of
Ferrara. The Countess Leonore Sanvitale harbors no adulterous
desire toward Tasso, but, as the painful contention arises, she sees
how the poet, the poem, and the poem's glory might be transferred to her and her husband's court. For her, Tasso becomes a
prize to be won and a possession to be acquired. For the Princess
Leonore d'Este, Tasso is a beloved, almost an adored, friend upon
whom she lavishes affection that is wholly fleshless and well-nigh
ethereal, without her so much as dreaming that such affection
might rouse in him a love of a more earthly kind. Yet, at the play's
beginning, the Duke's impatience for the poem has been only
good-humoredly expressed, Leonore's design is no more than a
subconscious wish, and the Princess honestly believes she has at
her side an ideal friend, but only a friend.

Thus the curtain reveals the two ladies in the serenest of moods
as they twine their wreaths in a corner of the sunny garden. The
Princess, significantly, has woven her wreath of the dark, glossy
leaves of the laurel, sacred to poets. Reverently now she sets it
upon the brow of Vergil, sublimest of poets, whose bust rests upon

a pedestal at one side of the garden corner. With equal significance Countess Leonore has woven a wreath of many-colored flowers, and, matching her companion's gesture, she now places her bright garland on the brow of Ariosto, the prince of urbane and courtly poets of recent times, whose bust stands at the opposite side of the garden corner. Distinction is thus made between spiritual and worldly, private and social, both in the ladies themselves and in the ideals of poetry.

Needless to say, the disaster that impends will not befall a wholly blameless man. Tasso's life before arrival at this court had not been without sorrow and distress, but those painful experiences are now safely past and largely submerged in his intense dedication to his art. He is grateful for all the benefactions he has received. He has come to look upon these courtly persons as his little family where he is loved and honored and appreciated. Unwittingly he has presumed himself their equal, or at least, within the sacred realm of art, their equivalent in value. He does not perceive that he is an instrument of Ducal policy as a winner of fame for the House of Este and that his poem is, in a sense, a commodity. He is too completely immersed in his poetic creation, too far astray in his land of dreams, to judge shrewdly of those around him. He fondly imagines that his friends sympathize with his every rapture and yet somehow perform their realistic lives and functions in addition to sharing his world. At times he has imposed upon them. His hypersensitive nature has led him on one occasion to imagine that his room had been rifled, or again that a servant had spied on him, and he has demanded that the Duke investigate those cases. It would bewilder and humiliate him to know that the attention granted to his complaints was indulgence, not without exasperation, as to a wayward child. Lost in his poetic concentration, he is unaware that he does not distinguish between inspiration and caprice, between an artist's fervor and a kind of selfish thoughtlessness. On the other hand, he does sense the immense disparity between his own sheltered and deedless life and the feats of valor of the heroic Crusaders that he is chronicling in his poem. The disparity troubles him profoundly. He longs for a vigorous life of action; secretly he believes himself capable of such a life. And finally, below the level of the conscious, there is the latent passion for his beloved Princess, whose Renaissance Platonism permits her, quite innocently, to speak to him of exalted love. In short, he moves about encased, as it were, in a rainbow globe through the curved and colored walls of which all realities are distorted.

All the irridescent hues of that magic cage are resplendent about him as he steps into our view. His poem has just been completed and he is intoxicated with his achievement. With exaltation and with seer-like dignity he enters the garden and presents the glorious gift of his manuscript volume to his lord the Duke and to the ladies, beholding in them, not the actual persons that they are, but heroic figures, larger than life, like those in his poem. Their pleasure and praise he misconstrues as perfect apprehension of his work and of his worth. When the Duke bids him be crowned with the laurel for Vergil's brow and by the hand of the beloved Princess herself, he is overwhelmed by such consecration. For a moment he is translated amid fire, while still in his mortal body, to the realms of the immortals.

It is worth noting that the visual aspects of this tableau are a vivid realization of the title-page engraving in the German version of *Jerusalem Delivered* which Goethe read as a boy. It is further worth noting that this dramatic moment will be recapitulated in Romantic terms thirty years later when, in Heinrich von Kleist's play, the Princess Natalie will hold out the wreath of fame to the Prince of Homburg.

Tasso is enraptured. From beloved hands he has received the wreath of renown from Vergil's head. The bestowal was ordered by the Duke, who must therefore be acknowledging him as an equal, or at least as of equivalent worth. That the bestowal was a whimsical gesture of mere social amiability on the part of the Duke never enters his mind. That the ladies concur in a pretty game is unthinkable to him. Nor does he perceive the gulf that divides friends' approval from the tested fame of centuries.

At this moment Antonio Montecatino arrives, a vigorous, prac-

tical man of affairs, fresh from victory in an astute battle of diplomatic wits in the world of hard reality. From his lips we hear first
the proper social greetings, then the forthright delivery of his
news to his sovereign, and he delivers his news not only with due
respect but with justifiable pride and a certain hearty relish,
directly, man to man. The Duke responds in kind, swiftly turning
his attention from poetic gift to diplomatic triumph. This is a
lucky day for him and his government. The ladies likewise give
all attention to Antonio. In the twinkling of an eye Tasso's poetic
apotheosis has been forgotten for a single worldly achievement.
When at last Antonio's attention is directed to the crowned laure-
ate he deems the whole scene to be contemptibly trivial, an idle
game played with home talent; he ignores the living successor to
Vergil and speaks at length in praise of Ariosto. Tasso stands
bewildered, confounded. Before Antonio, who robustly personi-
fies the non-poetic half of life, he must be mute for sheer lack of
anything to say.

At the beginning of Act II Tasso confesses to his beloved
Princess the great chagrin of that confrontation. She is aware of
her friend's chagrin. She is also aware that Tasso and Antonio
embody antithetical halves of life, and she urgently desires a uni-
fication of these antitheses. She persuades Tasso to take the initial
step toward a friendship with Antonio which can only result in
the two men's mutual advantage, concluding her persuasion with
the word "love" — in its Renaissance Platonic ambiguity. All the
irridescent hues of Tasso's magic cage glow once more. Within
his private reference the word "love" has kindled wild confidence
and wilder aspirations. Antonio comes. Tasso pours forth what he
believes to be the irresistable impassioned rhetoric of good will
and friendship. To his stupefaction he is answered by cool aloof-
ness and contempt. He invokes the Princess' will and command.
Antonio's rebuff becomes still sharper. The exchange comes to
outright quarrel, the quarrel waxes vehement, even to misconduct
toward the intervening Duke. Wild with resentment, Tasso retires
as bidden — to his room, like a misbehaving child.

One by one, Tasso's friends, including the apologetic Antonio, seek to repair the damage done. In vain. Irritation and dissension gradually bring to the fore those defects of character in each of them. To the youth's distraught sensitivities those defects become the true, hidden, and total characters of his friends so lately idealized. Where he saw saints and demigods before, he now sees rascals and demons. All the irrational impulses of his nature are now given free rein. In his murky hallucinations of treachery he himself now becomes treacherous, sly, and hateful, coming at last to screamed insults and to blasphemy against all friendship and all love. Before he has finished he has broken every tie of restraint, every bond of decency. In his frantic desire to wound as painfully as he has been wounded he lays waste every valuable compartment of his existence. When, with the ruin complete and his frenzy spent, he stands hopelessly before the spectacle of his self-destruction, he hears Antonio's words: he is a poet still. Like a bell tone the words recall him to himself. The gift of poetry remains intact amid the wreckage.

> And if men in their torment must be mute,
> A god gave me the power to tell my pain.

In total anguish he acknowledges his folly and his inability to cope with reality and he throws himself in despair upon the mercy of the man he hated most.

* * *

Half a lifetime after the publication of *Tasso,* J.-J. Ampère wrote in *Le Globe* for May 20, 1826:

> ". . . il me semble que c'est lui (i.e., Goethe) qui parle par la bouche du Tasse; et dans cette poésie si harmonieuse, si délicate, il y a du 'Werther.' "

And Goethe himself, speaking to Eckermann on May 3, 1827, acknowledged that Ampère had rightly judged *Tasso* as "an intensified *Werther.*" There are, however, significant differences between the two works. For instance, Werther's painting had served in secondary place to indicate his general sensitivity; it might be termed an attribute of the hero; his primary experience was a hopeless love. With Tasso, the love motif is secondary and

our attention is focused primarily upon his plight as a hypersensitive artist unable to deal with the actual world. In Goethe's
own words, as reported in a letter of Caroline Herder's to her
husband in March of 1789, the core of the drama is "the disproportion of talent to life."

Such a topic must forever appeal to fewer readers and spectators
than the story of a hopeless love, and *Tasso* has always had fewer
— and more discerning — admirers than *Werther*. The reason is
not solely the obvious one, that hundreds of human beings have
had some experience of unhappy love where only one may have
had experience of the "disproportion of talent to life," either in
himself or among his personal acquaintance. In this play, as in
any tale about an artist, there is always the nagging question: is
the hero's talent as great as the author expects us to believe? In
Bernard Shaw's *The Doctor's Dilemma* we must take the fictional
painter's genius on faith, on the author's say-so. In Somerset
Maugham's *The Moon and Sixpence* we may, justly or otherwise,
have recourse to viewing the canvases of Gauguin, whereupon,
depending upon our artistic education and our taste, we may
make up our own minds. But taste varies in individuals as in gen-
erations. In the case of Torquato Tasso we may set out to read
his long poem, *Jerusalem Delivered,* a sixteenth century palace
poet's stylized narrative about the Crusaders of 1100, only to find
it unattractive by our modern notions of history, religion, and
poetry. In point of fact, the historical Tasso and the actual
Jerusalem Delivered are less relevant to proper understanding of
the present play than are Goethe and the works of Goethe. And
yet, for all the autobiographical matter embedded in this drama,
Goethe's life and works are also irrelevant to our proper understanding.

For the fact of *this* Tasso's genius we must accept the author's
word. With that point granted, the rest of the play must stand or
fall according to its merits. It sturdily stands. Indeed, to our
twentieth century minds it appeals most poignantly in terms of the
theme of "non-communication." Five upright people, closely associated in long friendship, speak at length with one another amid

leisured ease — and understand nothing of what is said. The genius of the group sees his companions first as blessed half-gods, then as malignant spirits, both notions being equidistant from the truth. Nor have they any but the faultiest notion of him or of his art. The four inhabitants of "the real world" do not even judge each other rightly. Each of them lives within a private frame of reference almost to the degree that Tasso inhabits his rainbow cage of illusion. Each mistakes the social facet of personality for the total personality. None of them rises higher than pained embarrassment at the contention that arises in their midst, and, when the catastrophe is complete, only Antonio, the most worldly of them and the least intimate within their circle, has even a partially true understanding of what has happened.

Goethe's subjective experiences at the court of Weimar must, we reflect, have had their own poignancy in order to have so informed this poignant drama. He too was "a court poet" — though not quite with Tasso's degree of economic and political dependence — to a benevolent Duke, and he stood in just such an ambiguous love relationship with Charlotte von Stein as Tasso stood with the Princess Leonore d'Este. If specific models cannot be cited for the Countess Leonore Sanvitale and for Antonio Montecatino, persons like them may easily be imagined at the Weimar court. In fact, we may see in Antonio the projection of one aspect of Goethe's own personality, the aspect of the Prime Minister of the duchy, who could, on occasion, be efficient, stiffly correct, and coolly aloof, so that our play becomes, as in the case of Faust and Mephistopheles, a contention between hostile, antithetical selves of the author. For, though Goethe and Tasso were in significant degree congruent, they were by no means identical, any more than Goethe was identical with Werther. In real life Goethe did not shoot himself like Werther, nor did he collapse like Tasso, but he did, one day in 1786, set off precipitately for Italy without so much as a single farewell to his intimate associates of ten years. From Italy he wrote to them, but he did not return until 1788. By his own declaration those two Italian years constituted his "rebirth," and, once he did return, the "reborn" man made strikingly different disposition of his life and talents from what had previously been the case. The arrival of Christiane Vulpius under his roof, as his mistress, signaled a new epoch in his existence. The reader may decide for himself at what point spiritual autobiography in *Tasso* passes over into fiction. Certainly the play represents a valedictory to an era in the author's life.

En route for Italy, Goethe had various incomplete manuscripts in his luggage. There was a "completed" *Iphigenia in Tauris* in third draft and still unsatisfactory, as well as a prose draft of two acts of *Tasso,* not to mention works left unfinished from his pre-Weimar days such as *Egmont* and the set of vivid scenes that constituted the first work on *Faust.*

One by one he took them up beneath Italian skies. First, his already three-times-worked-over Greek play. By January of 1787 he had produced the fourth and final version, in blank verse, of *Iphigenia in Tauris.* There the author's dedicated, almost chivalric, submission to Frau von Stein resulted in the portrayal of a noble priestess who calmed her brother's madness, who exquisitely weighed all actions in the most delicate of ethical scales, and who drew all other characters upward after her as she herself advanced upward upon the ladder of ideal *humanitas.* The point should be stressed that Iphigenia embraced a *brother* with sisterly tenderness. But that play had been completed in its first draft as long ago as 1779 and only artistic formalities were being adjusted in 1786-87. The "problem" of the author's dedicated, almost chivalric, submission to Frau von Stein had, however, not yet been solved, or even fully debated in artistic form, and Goethe had a way of bringing realistic experiences to conclusion in artistic summary. We have a poem of Goethe's, addressed to Frau von Stein, in which he expresses his conviction that in a former lifetime she had been either his sister or his wife. (The lady was displeased by the poem.) Their former lifetime as brother and sister had been bodied forth in *Iphigenia in Tauris,* but the troublesome "or" of the poem still remained. A second play was a spiritual imperative for Goethe. Significantly, the Princess Leonore d'Este was not Tasso's sister in the second work, as Iphigenia had been the sister of Orestes in the first, but a woman free to marry,

and significantly Tasso desires her with an ardor about which
there is nothing fraternal. Moreover, the characters in the unfinished second play were less mellowly noble than in *Iphigenia,*
and their sharper, more "realistic" dissonances were to become
sharper still before the play was completed. The spell of Frau von
Stein had to be shattered before the work could be given the form
in which we have it. Not a few weeks or months, but four more
years were required to achieve that form.

The original notion of writing a Tasso play went back to 1780,
just after completion of the first draft of *Iphigenia in Tauris.*
Goethe's diary marks March 30, 1780 as "the inventive day" (der
erfindende Tag), though not until October 14th do we find the
diary entry: "Began to write *Tasso*." Letters to Frau von Stein
indicate work in progress through succeeding months. On March
25, 1781 he wrote her:

> Of *Tasso* there will be hardly any thinking today. Do you
> not notice, however, how love cares for your poet? For
> months the next scene was impossible for me, but how
> easily it will now flow from my heart.

Assuming that the allusion is to the colloquy between Tasso and
the Princess at the beginning of Act II, we may well ponder both
the fictional and the real-life situations. On April 20th he wrote
her that even as he began work on the play that morning "he wor-
shiped her," adding: "My entire soul is with you. . . . Today I
shall be diligent." Work continued through the summer of 1781.
Then inspiration faltered and we hear no more of the project
until 1787 and Rome.

The abandoned fragment was in prose (as the first draft of
Iphigenia had been). Its literary foundation was the markedly
uncritical biography of Torquato Tasso by Giovanni Battista
Manso, with its wholly fictional episode about the poet's unhappy
love for the Princess Leonore. That bit of Manso's manufactured
pathos was what had originally engaged Goethe's interest, and
from that nail he had spun his dramatic thread — which now
floated loose in air. Finally, and most important, the original plan
contained no Antonio Montecatino.

The years slipped by. The emotional stalemate of all artistic creativity became more and more irksome to Goethe, until that morning in 1786 when he abruptly set out for Italy without farewells. Within a month of completing the fourth and final version of *Iphigenia*, a letter of February 19, 1787 from Rome announced resumption of work on *Tasso*. Some five weeks later he took the boat from Naples to Palermo, and under the date of March 30, 1787 his *Italian Journey* chronicles the next step:

> Of all my papers I had taken along overseas only the first two acts of *Tasso*, written in poetic prose. These two acts, approximately equivalent to the present ones in plan and outline but composed ten years before, had about them something soft and nebulous, which soon vanished as I allowed the form to predominate according to more recent notions and allowed the rhythm to take over.

Under March 31st he mentions that the sea is running high and almost everyone on board is seasick. He, however, remained below decks, mulling the play over and over in his mind. On deck in the course of April 1st he felt the project clarifying itself like the weather around him, and on April 2nd he landed in Palermo with a sense that he was now master of the material which he had so carefully thought through while "in the whale's belly."

He reckoned too soon. Another whole year went by with nothing written. Back in Rome, under the date of February 1, 1788, he complained that the written portion of the play had to be redone; he could not bring himself to scrap the project altogether, nor could he be satisfied with the two acts as they stood, either in themselves or as a basis for continuation. In March, just a year after the voyage in "the whale's belly" when all had seemed so clear to him, he came upon the needed inspiration. He was now reading, he told the Duke of Weimar in a letter, the new biography of his Renaissance Italian poet by the Abbate Pierantonio Serassi, published in 1785. In this book the sentimental fictions of Manso yielded place to more realistic information. Tasso's political difficulties and his fear of the Inquisition were made clear. He stood as a man of his age, beset with obstacles and harried by prejudices. Most important of all, this book presented the character of Antonio Montecatino, under whose name Goethe collected traits of several of Tasso's opponents. The thread of Goethe's poetic thought no longer dangled in empty air; the loose end could now be firmly attached and from its firm line the elaborate dependent web of the total drama could now be spun.

Still there were delays. Autumn of 1788 brought Goethe back at last to Weimar. Some passages already in blank verse were read to Caroline Herder on October 6th, but progress was slow through the winter. A note sent early in the day of February 15, 1789 announced to a friend that the opening scene of the play had just been finished and that he would read the scene aloud at Frau von Stein's that afternoon. The four spring months of 1789 saw the steady composition of the final text. A letter of June 15th spoke of the work as being "in its last revision." Publication followed in 1790, in Volume 6 of a set of Goethe's collected works brought out by Göschen in Leipzig. In the author's own words, *Tasso* had indeed grown "like an orange tree, very slowly."

The simile of the orange tree indicates how closely Goethe associated his play with Italy — Italy, the land of art, of natural beauty, and of the fresh lease on life conferred uniquely upon him. He saw that southern land with aristocratic eyes as essentially a Renaissance and Baroque country, with noble remains of antiquity preserved across its landscape. Its medieval centuries interested him but little, and when he cried "Hellas!" he really had Italy in mind. To him, it was classical and neo-classical in one, and its spirit was precisely what he was trying to embody in *Tasso*. Yet, by a paradox that strikingly reveals the complexity of his mind, it was amid an Italian landscape, specifically the Borghese Gardens in Rome, that he composed the dark, transalpine grotesquerie of the Witch's Kitchen scene for *Faust*. There were undeclared reservations in his classical credo.

Hence we are not surprised at finding "irregularities" in his "Classical" play. *Tasso* has five acts, and it observes the unities of time and action, but it modifies the rule about unity of place by shifting its settings to various parts of the interior and environs of the pleasure-palace of Belriguardo. The verse is not a German adaptation of French alexandrine couplets but a German

adaptation of Shakespearean blank verse, here even more exquisitely musical and subtle than in *Iphigenia in Tauris*. A latter
eighteenth century awareness of nature finds expression in its text
in a way that would have surprised Racine. Subjective analysis
of character is pressed beyond what even *Bérénice* contained. The
persons of the drama are less august than those of French tragedy
of the seventeenth century, less exalted, less statuesque; we feel
them to be more nearly of normal life-size, more complexly mixed
of virtues and faults, more "realistic." The court of Ferrara could
not and does not approximate the grandeur of Greece and Rome.
The hero is not truly heroic, but of a problematic sensitivity:
". . . dans cette poésie si harmonieuse, si délicate, il y a du
'Werther.' " The secenario is a private invention of the author's,
and we sense it as interestingly new and not as a subtle reworking
of an older model in terms of the hallowed classical doctrine of
"imitation."

In short, the dramatic formula of Racine has been modified in
so many details that we discern in *Tasso* the portents of the
Romantic revolution soon to come in literature, even as the political revolution of 1789 was beginning just as the long-delayed composition was being brought to a close. *Tasso* is the last rose of
the neo-classical summer, a belated, unexpected, magnificent, final
bloom on the Racinian stock.

CHARACTERS

ALFONSO THE SECOND, DUKE OF FERRARA
LEONORE D'ESTE, SISTER OF THE DUKE
LEONORE SANVITALE, COUNTESS OF SCANDIANO
TORQUATO TASSO
ANTONIO MONTECATINO, SECRETARY OF STATE

The scene is at Belriguardo, a pleasure palace.
Time: around 1577.

Uniform with previous dramas by the present translator, scene numberings have been made according to the English system whereby only a shift of setting warrants a new scene, and not according to the continental system whereby the entrance or departure of a major character requires the indication of a new scene.

Since each Act of the present play represents continuous dialogue without shift of place, no scene divisions are indicated.

ACT I

A garden spot adorned with herms of the epic poets, downstage
right of Vergil, downstage left of Aristo.
The Princess. Leonore.

PRINCESS: You look at me and smile, Eleonore,
  And look back at yourself and smile again.
  What is the matter? Tell me as your friend.
  You seem bemused, and yet you seem quite pleased.
LEONORE: Oh yes, my Princess, I behold us both
  With pleasure here so rustically adorned.
  We look like truly happy shepherdesses,
  And we are busy, too, like happy ones.
  We're twining wreaths. Here, this one, bright with flowers,
  Keeps growing more and more beneath my hand.   10
  You, with your loftier mind and nobler heart,
  Chose for yourself the slender, fragile laurel.
PRINCESS: The branches I have woven in my thoughts,
  They have already found a worthy head.
  With gratitude I place them here on Vergil.
               (She crowns the bust of Vergil.)
LEONORE: Then I will set my own full, joyous wreath
  On Master Lodovico's lofty brow—
               (She crowns the bust of Ariosto.)
  Let him whose jests will never fade away
  Receive at once his share of this new springtime.
PRINCESS: It is obliging of my brother to   20
  Bring us so early out into the country.
  We can be by ourselves and dream our way
  For hours back to the poets' golden age.
  I love this Belriguardo, for I spent

3

Many a day of happy childhood here,
And this new greenness and this sunlight brings
Me back the feeling of that bygone time.
LEONORE: Oh yes, we find ourselves in a new world!
    The shade of these eternally green trees
    Already gladdens, and the murmur of   30
    These fountains quickens us anew to life.
    Young branches sway upon the morning wind.
    The flowers in the beds gaze up at us
    In friendly fashion with their childlike eyes.
    With confidence the gardener unroofs
    The hothouse for the oranges and lemons,
    The blue sky over us is in repose,
    And on the far horizon there the snow
    Of distant mountains melts to fragrant mist.
PRINCESS: The springtime would be very welcome to me   40
    If it did not deprive me of my friend.
LEONORE: Do not remind me in these gracious hours,
    O Princess, of how soon I must depart.
PRINCESS: Whatever you are leaving, you will find
    Again, and doubly, in that mighty city.
LEONORE: My duty summons me, love summons me
    Back to my husband, who has been so long
    Without me. I bring him his son, who has
    So swiftly grown this year, so swiftly formed,
    And I will share in his paternal joy.   50
    Florence is vast and splendid, but the worth
    Of all of its accumulated treasures
    Can never match Ferrara's precious jewels.
    The people made a city of that city,
    Ferrara gained its greatness through its princes.
PRINCESS: Through the good human beings rather, who
    By chance met here and for good fortune formed
    Alliances.
LEONORE: Chance scatters what chance gathers.
    A noble person will attract the noble

And can retain them firmly, as you do.   60
Around your brother and around yourself
Assemble minds that are quite worthy of you.
And you are worthy of your great forefathers.
Here was enkindled the fair light of learning,
With joy, and of emancipated thought,
When barbarism still enclosed the world
With heavy gloom. While I was yet a child
My ear rang with the names of Ércole
Of Este and Ippólito of Este.
Ferrara was, with Rome and Florence, much   70
Praised by my father! Many was the time
I yearned to go there; and now here I am.
Here Petrarch was received, here he was fostered,
And Ariosto found his models here.
No great name can be named by Italy
Which this house has not harbored as its guest.
And it is advantageous entertaining
A genius: if you give a gift to him,
He leaves a finer one behind for you.
The place where once a good man has set foot   80
Is consecrate; a hundred years thereafter
His word and deed resound unto the grandchild.
PRINCESS: Yes, if the grandchild warmly feels, as you do;
    I often envy you that happy fortune.
LEONORE: Which you enjoy serenely, purely, as
    Few others do. My full heart forces me
    To say straight off what I acutely feel;
    You feel it better, feel it deeply, and —
    Say nothing. Momentary seeming does
    Not dazzle you, sharp wit does not beguile you,   90
    And flattery glides vainly to your ear.
    Firm stands your mind and faultless your good taste,
    Your judgment true, your sympathy is great
    With greatness, which you know as your own self.
PRINCESS: You should not lend this supreme flattery

The raiment of the intimacy of friendship.

LEONORE: The friendship is quite just, and it alone
 Can know the total compass of your worth.
 Let me give opportunity and fortune
 Their share as well in your accomplishment;   100
 You have it, all the same, and such you are.
 And the whole world reveres you and your sister
 Before all the great women of your time.

PRINCESS: That, Leonore, can move me but little
 When I consider just how small one is,
 And what one is, one owes to other people.
 For my skill in the ancient languages
 And best things from times past, I thank my mother;
 Yet neither daughter ever was her equal
 In learning or in excellence of mind,   110
 And if one of us is to be compared
 With her, Lucretia surely has that right.
 I can assure you also that I never
 Regarded as a rank or a possession
 What Nature or what luck bestowed on me.
 When clever men discourse I am delighted
 That I can understand just what they mean.
 Let it be an opinion of a man
 Of ancient times and of his actions' worth,
 Or let some branch of learning be the topic   120
 Which by extension through experience
 Will profit human beings and uplift them:
 Wherever noble men's discourse may lead,
 I gladly follow, for I do so with ease.
 I like to hear disputes of clever men
 When speakers' lips with light grace play upon
 The forces which so cheerfully and yet
 So fearsomely bestir the human breast;
 Or when the princely eagerness for fame
 And aggrandizing of possession forms   130
 The thinker's theme, and when the fine astuteness

Of an astute man deftly set in motion,
Instead of cheating us, gives us instruction.
LEONORE: Then following that serious entertainment
Our ear and inner sense repose with pleasure
Upon the rhymes provided by the poet
Who with his gracious tones instills emotions
Of utmost loveliness into our souls.
Your lofty mind encompasses vast realms,
While I like best to dwell upon the island   140
Of poetry amid the laurel groves.
PRINCESS: In this fair land the myrtle tends to grow,
They have sought to assure me, more than all
The other trees. And though the Muses are
Full many, one more rarely seeks to gain
A friend and playmate from among their number
Than one is glad to meet the poet who
Seems to avoid and even flee from us
And seeks for something which we do not know
And which perhaps he does not know himself.   150
How nice, then, it would be if he should meet us
Some lucky hour and with sudden rapture
Discovered in us the treasure which he long
Had searched for and in vain through the wide world.
LEONORE: I must admit the justice of your jest,
It hits its mark in me, but not profoundly.
I honor every man and his true worth
And I am being only just to Tasso.
His vision scarcely tarries on this earth,
His ear perceives the harmony of Nature;   160
What history provides, what this life gives,
His heart at once and willingly takes up:
Things scattered far and wide his mind assembles
And his emotions give life to things lifeless.
He can ennoble what seemed base to us,
And things esteemed turn in his sight to naught.
Within this private magic circle walks

That admirable man and draws us on
To walk with him and share experiences.
He seems to come close to us, yet remains   170
Afar; he seems to look at us, and spirits
May strangely stand before him in our stead.
PRINCESS: You have described the poet well and fondly
Who hovers in the realm of his sweet dreams.
I feel, however, that reality
Attracts him strongly too, and holds him fast.
Those lovely songs which we from time to time
Discover fastened to our trees and which,
Like golden apples, make a fragrant, new
Hesperia, do you not recognize   180
Them all for gracious fruits of a true love?
LEONORE: I too take pleasure in those lovely pages.
And with his diverse mind he glorifies
A single picture throughout all his rhymes.
At times he lifts it up in shining glory
Unto the starry sky, himself adoring
Like angels over clouds before the picture;
Then he pursues it through the quiet meadows,
Entwining every flower in his garland.
If the adored one leaves, he consecrates   190
The path that her fair foot has lightly trodden.
Concealed in thickets like the nightingale,
He fills the grove and air with harmonies
Of his laments poured from his lovesick heart.
His charming grief, the blessed melancholy
Entices every ear, all hearts must follow —
PRINCESS: And if he were to name his subject, he
Would call it by the name of Leonore.
LEONORE: That is your name as much as it is mine.
I would resent it if it were another.   200
I am delighted that he can conceal
His feeling for you in that double meaning.
And I am pleased that he remembers me

Amid the gracious sounding of that name.
There is no question here of any love
That seeks to be the master of its object,
Or would exclusively possess it and
In jealousy forbid its view to others.
When in his blissful contemplation he
Concerns himself with your worth he may also   210
Take his delight in my own slighter person.
He does not love us, — pardon my so speaking!
From all the spheres he conjures what he loves
Down into the one name which we both bear
And he communicates his feelings to us;
We seem to love the man, and we love only
In him the highest things that we can love.

PRINCESS: You have gone very deeply, Leonore,
Into this science, and you tell me things
Which almost touch upon my ear alone   220
And scarcely penetrate into my soul.

LEONORE: What? You, a Plato scholar, and not grasp
What a mere novice dares to prattle of?
It must be that I have too gravely erred.
And yet I am not wholly wrong, I know.
Amid this gracious school Love does not show
Himself, as formerly, as a spoiled child;
He is the youth who wed with Psyche and
Who in the privy-council of the gods
Has seat and voice. He does not rage so wanton   230
From one heart to another, back and forth.
He does not seize straight off on form and beauty
With sweet misjudgment, and he does not pay
For sudden rapture with disgust and loathing.

PRINCESS: Here comes my brother. Let us not betray
The turn our conversation took again.
We would have to endure his joking, as
Our costume met his mockery before.
                    (Enter Alfonso.)

ALFONSO: I have been looking everywhere for Tasso
   And do not find him — even here with you.   240
   Can you not give me any news of him?
PRINCESS: I saw him little yesterday, and not
   At all today.
ALFONSO: It is his long-time failing
   To seek seclusion more than company.
   If I forgive him for avoiding motley
   Throngs of people and preferring to
   Commune in quiet freely with his mind,
   I still can not approve that he avoids
   The very circle which his friends comprise.
LEONORE: If I am not in error, you will soon,   250
   O Prince, transmute your blame to gladsome praise.
   I saw him from afar today; he had
   A book and tablet, wrote, and paced, and wrote.
   A hurried word that he spoke yesterday
   Seemed to announce to me his work's completion.
   He troubles only with correcting small points
   To lay a worthy offering at last
   Before your grace, which has done so much for him.
ALFONSO: He shall be welcome *when* he brings it, and
   Acquitted for a long, long time to come.   260
   Much as I sympathize with his long efforts,
   Much as the great work pleases me and must
   Please me in many ways, nevertheless
   My own impatience is increasing too.
   He can not finish it, can not get through;
   He keeps on changing, slowly moves ahead.
   Stops once again, and keeps on cheating hopes.
   One is indignant seeing pleasure that
   One thought so near postponed to times remote.
PRINCESS: But I praise the discretion and the care   270
   With which he moves step by step to his goal.
   By favor of the Muses only will
   So many rhymes shape firmly to a whole!

And his soul cherishes this impulse only:
His poem must be rounded to a whole.
He will not heap up tale on pretty tale
That entertain delightfully and then
Like empty words delude and fade away.
Leave him alone, my brother. Time is not
The measure of a work of quality.   280
And if posterity is to enjoy it,
The artist's own times must forget themselves.

ALFONSO: Let us, dear sister, work together here,
As we have often done to our advantage.
If I am over-zealous, mitigate;
And if you are too mild, I will press harder.
Thus we perhaps will see him all at once
At the goal where we have so long desired him.
And then the fatherland and all the world
Will be astounded at the work achieved.   290
I shall have my own share in the renown,
And he will be inducted into life.
A noble man cannot owe his formation
To any narrow circle. Fatherland
And world at large must have effect on him.
He must learn to endure both praise and blame.
He must be forced to know himself and others
Aright. Seclusion will no longer lull him
With praise. Foes *will* not and friends *may* not spare him.
The youth will then exert his strength in struggle,   300
Feel what he is, and soon perceive his manhood.

LEONORE: Then you will still do everything for him,
My Lord, as you already have done much.
A talent forms itself in solitude,
A character amid the stream of life.
O may he form his spirit like his art
On your instruction, and may he no longer
Shun human beings, and may his suspicion
Be not transformed at last to fear and hatred!

ALFONSO: Only one who does not know human beings   310
   Will fear them, and a man who shuns them will
   Misjudge them. Such is his case, and by stages
   A free mind comes to be perplexed and chained.
   Thus he is often vastly more concerned
   About my favor than beseems him, and
   He has mistrust of many who, I know,
   Are not his enemies. If it bechances
   A letter goes astray, or a domestic
   Transfers from his own service to some other,
   Or if a paper gets out of his hands,   320
   Immediately he sees design, betrayal,
   And malice undermining his own fate.
PRINCESS: Let us, beloved brother, not forget
   A man can not get outside of himself.
   And if a friend upon a walk with us
   Should hurt his foot, we would prefer to walk
   More slowly and extend our hand to him
   Gladly and willingly.
ALFONSO: It would be better
   If we could heal him and were rather to
   Try out at once a cure upon a surgeon's   330
   Reliable advice, and then proceed
   On the new path of fresh life with the cured man.
   And yet, my dear ones, I hope never to
   Take on myself the guilt of the harsh surgeon.
   I'm doing what I can to inculcate
   His heart with confidence and with assurance.
   I frequently give him decisive signs
   Of favor before many people. If
   He makes complaint to me, I have it seen to,
   As I did do when recently he thought   340
   His room was burglarized. If nothing is
   Then found, I show him calmly how I see it.
   And since one must use every means, I practice
   Patience, as he does deserve, with Tasso.

And you, I know, both willingly support me.
I have now brought you to the country and
Myself return this evening to the city.
You will just for a moment see Antonio;
He comes from Rome to fetch me. We have much
To settle and discuss. Decisions must   350
Be made, and many letters must be written.
All these things force me back into the city.
PRINCESS: Will you allow us to accompany you?
ALFONSO: Remain in Belriguardo, go together
  Over to Consandoli. Enjoy
  The lovely days entirely at your leisure.
PRINCESS: You cannot stay with us? Can the affairs
  Not be done here as well as in the city?
LEONORE: You take Antonio away at once
  Who would have had so much to tell of Rome?   360
ALFONSO: It won't do, children. But I will come back
  With him as soon as possible, and then
  He shall recount to you, and you shall help
  Me in rewarding him, who once again
  Has made such great exertions in my service.
  And once we have got our discussions over,
  Then let the swarm come in, so things will be
  Gay in our gardens, and a beauteous lady,
  If I should seek one, may be glad to meet
  Me also, as is fitting, in the coolness.   370
LEONORE: We'll look the other way quite cheerfully.
ALFONSO: And yet you know that I can be indulgent.
PRINCESS (looking off stage):
  I have been watching Tasso coming. Slowly
  He moves his steps, then stops at intervals
  All of a sudden as if undecided,
  Then comes on faster toward us, and then stops
  Again.
ALFONSO: If he is thinking and composing
  Do not disturb his dreams and let him walk.

LEONORE: No, he has seen us, he is coming here.

(Enter Tasso with a book bound
in parchment.)

TASSO: I come up slowly to present a work,   380
And still am hesitant to give it to you.
Too well I know it still remains unfinished
However much it might seem to be ended.
But though I was concerned about presenting
It to you uncompleted, new concern
Compels me now: I should not like to seem
Too anxious, nor to seem ungrateful either.
And as a man can only say: "Here am I!"
So friends considerately will rejoice,
So I can only say: "Accept it now!"   390

(He presents the volume.)

ALFONSO: You quite surprise me with your gift and make
This lovely day a festival for me.
And so at last I hold it in my hands
And call it in a certain sense my own!
I long have wished you might make up your mind
And finally tell me: "Here! It is enough."

TASSO: If you are satisfied, then it is finished;
For it belongs to you in every sense.
If I considered all the effort spent,
If I looked at the ink-strokes of my pen,   400
Then I might well declare: "This work is mine."
But if I look more closely at what gives
This poem dignity and inner value,
I see that I have it from you alone.
If Nature kindly gave me the fair gift
Of poetry from generous caprice,
Capricious Fortune had thrust me away
From her with fierce and wrathful violence;
And if the fair world had resplendently
With all its plenitude caught the boy's gaze,   410
My youthful mind had early been beclouded

By my dear parents' undeserved privation.
If ever my lips opened up to sing,
It was a mournful song that poured from them
And I accompanied with my gentle tones
My father's sorrow and my mother's anguish.
And it was you alone who raised me up
Out of a narrow life to lovely freedom,
Who lifted every care off of my head
And gave me liberty so that my soul   420
Was able to expand in valiant song.
Whatever praise my work may now obtain
I owe to you, for it belongs to you.

ALFONSO: A second time you merit every praise
And tactfully honor both yourself and us.

TASSO: Could I but say what I acutely feel,
That what I bring I have from you alone!
The youth of no achievements — could he have drawn
This poem from himself? The shrewd direction
Of lively warfare — did he think that up?   430
The art of weapons mightily displayed
By every hero on the day appointed,
The captain's sense, the bravery of knights,
How vigilance and cunning are subdued,
O did you not inspire all that in me,
My wise and valiant Prince, as if you were
My Genius who could take delight in making
His high, his unattainably high being
Manifest through a mere mortal man?

PRINCESS: Enjoy the work now which gives us delight.   440

ALFONSO: Rejoice in every good man's approbation.

LEONORE: Rejoice now in your universal fame.

TASSO: For me there is sufficient in this moment.
I thought of you alone as I reflected
And wrote; to please you was my highest wish,
To entertain you was my furthest goal.
One who does not see the world in his friends

Does not deserve to have the world hear of him.
Here is my fatherland, here is the circle
In midst of which my soul is glad to dwell.   450
Here I give ear, here I note every hint.
Here speaks experience, erudition, taste,
I see world and posterity before me.
The masses make an artist shy and muddled;
Only those like you, who understand
And feel, they shall alone judge and reward!
ALFONSO: If we stand for world and posterity,
It is not seemly merely to receive.
The splendid token that rewards a poet,
Which even heroes, who have need of him,   460
Unenvying behold upon his head,
I see right here upon your forebear's brow.
                    (pointing to the herm of Vergil.)
Was it a genius or coincidence
That wove and brought it? Not for nothing does
It chance to be here. I hear Vergil say:
"Why honor ye the dead? They had their joy
And their reward while they were still alive.
Now if you so admire and reverence us,
Then give unto the living ones their share.
My marble image has been crowned enough: 470
These verdant branches should belong to life."
        *(Alfonso beckons to his sister; she takes the
        wreath from the bust of Vergil and approaches
        Tasso. He falls back.)*
LEONORE: What? You refuse? But see whose hand presents you
The beautiful, imperishable wreath!
TASSO: O let me hesitate! I do not see
How I can ever live beyond this hour.
ALFONSO: In the enjoyment of the fine possession
Which frightens you for the initial moment.
PRINCESS *(as she holds the wreath aloft):*
You grant me the unwonted pleasure, Tasso,

Of saying to you wordless what I think.

TASSO: Kneeling I accept the lovely burden   480
    From your dear hands upon my feeble head.
               (He kneels; the Princess places
                   the wreath upon him.)

LEONORE *(applauding):*
    Long live the poet for the first time crowned!
    O how the wreath befits the modest man!
                  (Tasso stands up.)

ALFONSO: It is the symbol merely of the crown
    That shall adorn you on the Capitol.

PRINCESS: And up there louder voices will acclaim you;
    Here friendship gives reward with gentle lips.

TASSO: O take it off my head again, take it
    Away! It scorches every lock of hair,
    And like a ray of sunlight that might strike   490
    Too hot upon my head, it burns the power
    Of thought out of my brow. A heat of fever
    Excites my blood. Forgive! It is too much!

LEONORE: This branch affords protection rather to
    The man's head who must walk amid the fervent
    Regions of renown, and cools his brow.

TASSO: I am not worthy of the coolness which
    Should only blow upon the brows of heroes.
    O raise it up, ye gods, transfigure it
    Among the clouds so that it floats on high   500
    And higher out of reach! so that my life
    May be eternal progress toward that goal!

ALFONSO: Achieving early, one learns early to
    Esteem the fair possessions of this life.
    Enjoying early, one will not by choice
    In this life do without what he once had;
    And once possessing, one must be in armor.

TASSO: And donning armor one must feel within
    His heart a strength that never will desert him.
    Ah, it deserts me even now! In fortune   510

It fails me now, the innate strength that bade me
Steadfastly meet misfortune and with pride
Confront injustice. Has my joy dissolved,
And has the rapture of the present moment
Dissolved the very marrow in my limbs?
My knees collapse beneath me! Once again
You see me bowed, O Princess, down before you.
Hear, then, my plea and take the wreath away
So that, as though awakened from a dream
Of beauty I may feel a life new-quickened.   520

PRINCESS: If you can quietly and humbly bear
The talent which the gods have given you,
Then learn to bear these branches also, for
They are the finest thing that we can give you.
The head which they have once touched worthily,
About that brow they will forever hover.

TASSO: Then let me go away in shame. Within
The deep grove let me hide my happiness,
As formerly I hid my sorrows there.
There I will walk alone, no eye will there   530
Remind me of my undeserved good fortune.
And if by chance a lucid fountain shows
Me there a man in its pure mirror, resting
In thought and oddly crowned in the reflection
Of sky between the trees, between the rocks,
Then it will seem as if I were beholding
Elysium upon that magic surface
Created. I will ponder and inquire:
Now who may this departed spirit be?
The youth of ancient times? Engarlanded   540
So fair? Who will tell me his name? His merits?
A long time I will wait and think: If only
Another one and still another would
Come and join him in friendly conversation!
O to behold the heroes and the poets
Of ancient times assembled by this fountain,

O to behold them here inseparable
Forever as in life they were united!
Thus by its power does the magnet join
Things iron with things iron fast together   550
As equal striving joins heroes and poets.
Homer forgot himself, and his whole life
Was consecrated to thought of two men,
And Alexander in Elysium
Makes haste to seek out Homer and Achilles.
O if I only might be present to
Behold those souls supreme united then!

LEONORE: Awake! Awake! And do not make us feel
    You fail to recognize the present time.

TASSO: It is the present time that so exalts me.   560
    I only seem far off, I am enraptured!

PRINCESS: I am delighted, when you speak with spirits,
    To hear you talk so humanly with them.

       (A page steps up to the Prince and quietly
       delivers something.)

ALFONSO: He has arrived, right at the best of times.
    Antonio! — Bring him here. — Ah, here he comes.

             (Enter Antonio.)

    Welcome! who bring good news and your own self
    At one and the same time.

PRINCESS: Our greetings to you!

ANTONIO: I hardly dare to say what satisfaction
    Gives me a new existence in your presence.
    In your sight I again find everything   570
    That I so long have missed. You seem to be
    Pleased with what I have done and have accomplished,
    Thus I have my reward for every care,
    For many a day endured now with impatience
    And wasted now deliberately. We have,
    Then, what we want, and there is no more quarrel.

LEONORE: My greetings to you also, angry as
    I am. You come just when I have to leave.

ANTONIO: So that my good luck may not be quite perfect
    You take a lovely part away at once!   580
TASSO: My greetings also! I too hope joy from
    The presence of the much experienced man.
ANTONIO: You'll find me genuine if ever you
    Choose to look over from your world to mine.
ALFONSO: Although you have informed me in your letters
    Of what you did and how things fared with you,
    I still have many things to ask about
    And by what means the business was accomplished.
    Upon that strange and wonderful terrain one's step
    Must be well gauged if it is finally   590
    To lead you to your proper purposes.
    A man who bears in mind his lord's advantage
    Will have no easy time of it in Rome;
    For Rome takes everything but gives you nothing,
    And if one goes there to get something, he
    Gets nothing, unless he in turn gives something,
    And he is lucky if he gets it then.
ANTONIO: It is not my demeanor or my skill
    Whereby I carried out your will, my Lord.
    What shrewd man would not find his master in   600
    The Vatican? No, many things concurred
    Which I could turn to our advantage. Gregory
    Respects and greets you and sends you his blessing.
    The aged man, the noblest on whose head
    A crown's weight ever lay, recalls with joy
    When he embraced you with his arm. The man
    Discriminant of men knows you and values
    You highly. And for your sake he did much.
ALFONSO: I am glad of his good opinion in
    So far as it is honest. But you know   610
    That one sees kingdoms lying small enough
    Before one's feet down from the Vatican,
    Not to speak of mortal men and princes.
    Just mention what it was that helped you most.

ANTONIO: Good! if you wish: the Pope's own lofty mind.
    For he sees small things small and great things great.
    In order that he may control a world
    He yields with friendly good will to his neighbors.
    The strip of land that he surrenders to you,
    He knows its worth, like the worth of your friendship.   620
    There must be calm in Italy, he wants
    To see friends close to home, keep peace along
    His borders, so the might of Christendom,
    Which he controls with power, may destroy
    Both Turks and heretics on either side.
PRINCESS: And are the men known whom he favors more
    Than others, who in confidence approach him?
ANTONIO: Experienced men alone possess his ear,
    And only energetic ones his favor
    And confidence. He, who from youth had served   630
    The state, controls it now and influences
    Those courts which years before he saw and knew
    As Nuncio and frequently directed.
    The whole world lies as clear before his gaze
    As the advantages of his own state.
    To see him operate is to admire him
    And be glad when the world discovers what
    He long has quietly prepared and managed.
    There is no finer sight in all the world
    Than to behold a Prince astutely ruling,   640
    Or see a realm where all obey with pride,
    Where each man thinks to serve himself alone
    Because he is asked only to do right.
LEONORE: How ardently I long to see that world
    Just once close by!
ALFONSO: But surely to work in it?
    For Leonore will not just look on.
    It would be very nice, my friend, however,
    If we could sometimes also get our hands
    Into the mighty game— Is that not so?

LEONORE *(to Alfonso):*
  You want to tease me, but you won't succeed.   650
ALFONSO: I owe you a great deal from other days.
LEONORE: Today I will remain, then, in your debt.
  Forgive me, and do not interrupt my questions.
                  (to Antonio)
  Has he done much to help his relatives?
ANTONIO: He has done neither less nor more than proper.
  A man of power who does not look after
  His own will be condemned, and by the people
  Themselves. With quiet moderation Gregory
  Knows how to use his relatives who serve
  The state as honest men, and thus fulfills   660
  With one concern two allied obligations.
TASSO: Does learning and does art likewise enjoy
  Protection from him? Does he emulate
  The mighty princes of the ancient time?
ANTONIO: He honors learning as far as it is
  Of use to rule the state, make peoples known;
  Art he esteems as far as it adorns
  And glorifies his Rome, makes palaces
  And temples works of wonder on this earth.
  Nothing must be superfluous around him!   670
  To pass, a thing must serve and be effective.
ALFONSO: And do you think that we can finish up
  The business soon? no further obstacles
  Will be presented to us here and there?
ANTONIO: I would be much deceived if this dispute
  Were not directly settled and forever
  Just by your signature and a few letters.
ALFONSO: Then I will praise these days of my life now
  As a time of advantage and good fortune.
  I see my boundaries enlarged and know   680
  Them safe for times to come. This you have managed
  Without a clash of swords, for which you well
  Deserve a civic crown. And that our ladies

Shall weave you from the nearest oak-leaves and
Emplace it on your brow this lovely morning.
Meanwhile, Tasso has enriched me also:
He has now won Jerusalem for us
And thus put modern Christendom to shame,
By cheerful courage and severe exertion
Attaining a remote and lofty goal. 690
And for his efforts you behold him crowned.

ANTONIO: You solve a riddle for me. With amazement
I noticed two men crowned as I arrived.

TASSO: If you see my good fortune with your eyes,
I only wish that with the very same
Glance you might look upon my spirit's shame.

ANTONIO: I long have known Alfonso is excessive
In his rewards, and you discover now
What all his people long ago discovered.

PRINCESS: When once you find out what he has achieved 700
You will see we are just and moderate.
We are the first and silent witnesses
Of the applause the world will not deny him
And future years will grant him ten times over.

ANTONIO: Through you he can be certain of his fame.
Who would presume to doubt when you give praise?
But tell me who has set this wreath upon
The brow of Ariosto?

LEONORE: My hand did so.

ANTONIO: That was well done! It decks him beautifully;
The laurel's self would not so well adorn him. 710
As Nature decks her inwardly rich heart
With garb of green and motley color, he
Garbs everything that can make human creatures
Worthy of respect and of affection
In flowery raiment of his fable-fiction.
Contentment, wisdom, and experience,
And mental vigor, taste, and pure sense for
The truly good, these in his poems seem,

In spirit and in person also, to
Repose as under flower-bearing trees,   720
Enfolded in the snow of the light blossoms,
Enwreathed with roses, whimsically ringed around
With wanton magic play of Amoretti.
The spring of plenty bubbles close at hand
With view of many-colored wondrous fishes.
The air is filled with rarities of fowl,
As copse and meadow are with unknown herds;
Roguishness half concealed in verdure listens,
From time to time out of a golden cloud
Wisdom intones exalted maxims, while   730
Upon a well-tuned lute wild madness seems
To rage about, now one way, now another,
And yet hold temperately to faultless rhythm.
Whoever ventures up beside this man
Deserves the wreath for sheer audacity.
Forgive me if I seem myself possessed
And, like a man in ecstasy, can not
Take heed of time or place or what I speak;
For all these poets, all these wreaths, the festive
And rare array of lovely ladies, they   740
Transport me from myself to a strange land.
PRINCESS: A man who can so well appreciate
One merit will not fail to see the other.
Some day you shall point out in Tasso's songs
What we have felt but only you perceived.
ALFONSO: Antonio, come along! I still have much
To ask about which I am curious.
And then till set of sun you shall be at
The ladies' disposition. Come! Farewell.   (749)
                    (Antonio follows the Prince,
                        Tasso, the ladies.)

ACT II

A room.
The Princess. Tasso.

TASSO: My steps pursue you with uncertainty,   750
    O Princess, and within my soul thoughts rise
    Without proportion and coherent order.
    Seclusion seems to beckon me and whisper
    Complaisantly: "Come and I will resolve
    The newly risen doubts within your breast."
    But if I cast a glance at you, or my
    Attentive ear hears one word from your lips,
    Then I feel a new daylight all around me
    And all my fetters fall away from me.
    I will confess to you that the man who   760
    Came to us unexpectedly did not
    Wake me with gentleness from my fair dream.
    His manner and his words affected me
    In such a wondrous way that more than ever
    I feel myself divided and again
    Am in confusing conflict with myself.
PRINCESS: It is impossible that an old friend
    Who has long led an alien life far off
    Should at the moment when he comes back to us
    Be found precisely as he was before.   770
    He has not altered in his inner self.
    Allow us a few days to live with him
    And then the strings will gradually be tuned
    Until felicitously a harmony
    Is realized again. If he then comes
    To know more closely what you have achieved

25

In all this time he certainly will place
You up beside the poet whom he now
Opposes to you as a towering giant.

TASSO: The praise of Ariosto from his lips,   780
My Princess, caused me more delight than it
Could have offended me. It is a comfort
For us to have praise lavished on a man
Who stands before us as a mighty model.
In quiet heart we can say to ourselves:
If you achieve a portion of his merit
A portion of his fame can not escape you.
No, what disturbs my heart within its depths,
What even now fills up my entire soul,
Were those forms of that other world which circles,   790
Alive, unresting, and tremendous, there
Around one great, uniquely subtle man
In orderly completion of the orbit
Which that demigod has dared assign it.
I harkened eagerly and heard with pleasure
The assured words of the experienced man.
Alas, the more I harkened, more and more
I foundered there before myself, I feared
That I would vanish on those rocks like Echo,
And like a mere non-entity be lost.   800

PRINCESS: And yet so short a time before you felt
How heroes and poets live for one another,
How heroes and poets seek out one another,
And neither needs feel envy of the other?
The feat that merits song is admirable,
But it is also fine to bring abundance
Of feats to future times through worthy songs.
Content yourself with gazing on the world's
Wild course, as from a shore, out from the safety
Of one small state that grants you its protection.   810

TASSO: Did I not with amazement first see here
How splendidly the brave man is rewarded?

I came here as an inexperienced boy
At a time when one festival upon
Another seemed to make Ferrara mid-point
Of the earth. O what a sight it was!
The spacious square whereon skilled Valor was
To show itself in all its glory formed
A circle such that it is hardly likely
The sun will shine upon a second time.   820
Here sat the fairest ladies in a throng,
And in a throng the first men of our age.
One's gaze ran through the noble crowd with wonder,
Exclaiming: "All these the fatherland has sent here,
That single, narrow land surrounded by
The sea. And they together constitute
The most illustrious court that ever sat
In judgment over honor, worth, and virtue.
Go through them one by one, you will find none
Of whom his neighbor needs to be ashamed!" —   830
And then the barriers were all thrown open.
Then horses stamped and shields and helmets gleamed,
Then grooms thronged in, then trumpet fanfares rang,
And lances shattered with a splitting sound,
Helmets and shields with blows resounded, dust
Swirling enveloped for a moment both
The victor's glory and the vanquished's shame.
O let me draw a curtain over all
That far too brilliant spectacle so that
Before that splendid sight my own unmerit   840
May not be too intensely clear to me.
PRINCESS: Although that noble circle and those feats
Enflamed you then for toil and emulation,
I still could certify for you, young friend,
At that same time the quiet creed of patience.
Those festivals you praise, and which were praised
To me at that time by a hundred tongues,
And many years since then, I did not see.

Off in a quiet place to which the furthest
Echo of joy could fade away with scarcely   850
An interruption, I had to endure
Much pain and many grievous thoughts as well.
With wings outspread Death's image hovered there
Before my eyes and blocked the prospect outward
Into the world that is forever new.
Only by slow degrees did it withdraw
And let me glimpse, as through a veil, the many
Hues of life, all wan, but grateful still.
I saw its vivid figures gently stir again
And when I stepped forth, still supported by   860
My ladies, for the first time from my sick-room,
There came Lucretia full of joyous life
And with her hand presented you to me.
You were the first in that new life of mine
To meet me, new and quite unknown before.
I had great hopes for you and me; that hope
Has up to now not disappointed us.

TASSO: And I, bewildered by the tumult of
The surging throng, bedazzled with such splendor,
And agitated by hosts of emotions,   870
Walked silently along beside your sister
Through the tranquil hallways of the palace,
Then stepped into the room where you appeared
Before us presently supported by
Your ladies— What a moment! O forgive me!
As one bewitched by frenzy and delusion
Is lightly healed by presence of a godhead,
So I was cured of all my fantasies,
Of all my mania, of every false
Impulsion, by one glance into your gaze.   880
If raw desires had formerly been lost
In the pursuing of a thousand objects,
I now stepped back within myself for shame
And came to know that which is worth desiring.

Thus one may search the wide sands of the sea
In vain to find a pearl that lies enclosed
And hidden in the quiet of a shell.
PRINCESS: It was a lovely time that then began,
And had my sister not wed the Duke of
Urbino and removed from us, years would   890
Have flown by in untroubled happiness.
Unfortunately we now too greatly miss
The cheerful mind, the heart replete with courage
And life, the rich wit of that gracious woman.
TASSO: I realize, and all too well, that since
The day of her departure no one could
Make up for you the pure delight you lost.
How often it has wrenched my heart! How often
I told the quiet grove my grief for you!
"Alas!" I cried, "Her sister has sole right,   900
Sole fortune to be precious to this dear one?
Is there no other heart in whom she might
Confide, no other soul of equal temper
With hers? Have mind and wit been quite extinguished?
Was this one woman, excellent as she was,
All things in all?" O pardon me, my Princess!
I often thought then of myself and wished
I might mean something to you. Very little,
Yet something, not with words, but with my actions
I wished to be so, show you by my life   910
Just how my heart was vowed to you in secret.
But I did not succeed, and far too often,
Through error, I did things that caused you pain,
Outraged the man to whom you gave protection,
Confused unwisely what you wished resolved,
And always at the moment when I wanted
To come more near, felt far and farther off.
PRINCESS: I have not, Tasso, ever failed to see
Your true intent, and I know you are zealous
In working your own harm. But where my sister   920

Could get along with anyone soever,
You scarcely seem to make out with a friend,
Not even after many years.
TASSO: Condemn me!
   But tell me then where is the man or woman
   Whom I may venture to address and talk to
   With free heart as I dare to talk to you?
PRINCESS: You should do more confiding in my brother.
TASSO: He is my Prince! — But do not think that any
   Wild impetus to freedom swells my bosom.
   Man is not born so that he may be free.   930
   And for a noble one no happiness
   Is finer than to serve a Prince whom he
   Reveres. He is my Lord, and I perceive
   The total compass of that lofty word.
   I must learn to be silent when he speaks,
   And do as he commands, no matter how
   Intensely heart and judgment contradict him.
PRINCESS: But with my brother that is not the case.
   And now we have Antonio back again,
   You are sure of a new and clever friend.   940
TASSO: I had so hoped; now I despair of it
   Almost. How profitable association
   With him would have been for me, and how useful
   His counsel in a thousand instances!
   He has, I dare say, all I lack. Yet — though
   All gods conjoined to bring gifts to his cradle,
   Unfortunately the Graces stayed away,
   And one who lacks gifts from those gracious ones
   May well own much, may well give much away,
   But none can ever rest upon his bosom.   950
PRINCESS: Yet he may be confided in, and that
   Is much! You must not ask for everything
   From one man, and he does what he has promised.
   Once he declares himself to be your friend,
   He will provide whatever you may lack.

You two must be allied! I will be pleased
To bring this thing about before too long.
Only, do not resist, as is your habit.
Thus we have long had Leonore here,
Who is refined and lovely and with whom   960
It is not hard to get along, yet you
Have not been close to her as she desired.

TASSO: I have obeyed you, otherwise I would
Have held aloof instead of going nearer.
As amiable as she appears to be,
I don't know how it is, I rarely could
Be wholly frank with her, and even when
It is her purpose to please friends, one senses
The purpose and one is put off by it.

PRINCESS: On this path, Tasso, we shall never find   970
Companionship! This path leads us astray
To wander on through solitary thickets
And silent valleys; more and ever more
The personality is spoiled and seeks
To reestablish in its inner being
The golden age which it finds lacking outside,
However little this attempt succeeds.

TASSO: O what a term my Princess there expresses!
The golden age, O whither has it fled?
For which all hearts in vain are filled with yearning!   980
When on the free earth human beings roamed
Abroad in their enjoyment like the happy herds;
When a primaeval tree on bright-hued meadow
Afforded shade for shepherdess and shepherd,
And younger shrubs entwined their tender branches
Familiarly about a yearning love;
Where clear and still on sand forever pure
The supple stream embraced the nymphs so softly;
Where in the grass the startled serpent vanished
Quite harmlessly, where the audacious faun,   990
Soon chastised by the doughty youth, took flight;

Where every bird in freedom of the air
And every beast through hill and valley roving
Told man: Whatever pleases is allowed.
PRINCESS: My friend, the golden age is doubtless past,
But good men will establish it anew.
And if I may state how I understand it:
The golden age with which the poet often
Beguiles us, that same golden age existed,
It seems to me, as little then as now.   1000
And if it did exist, it surely was
What may recur repeatedly for us,
For kindred hearts still chance on one another
And share enjoyment of the lovely world.
But in the motto one word must be changed,
My friend: What is befitting is allowed.
TASSO: O if a general court consisting solely
Of good and noble human beings would
Decide what is befitting; and not have
Each man deem proper what is useful to him.   1010
We see how for the mighty and the clever
All thrives, and he permits himself all things.
PRINCESS: If you would learn precisely what is fitting,
Do no more than inquire of noble women.
It is above all others their concern
That everything that happens is befitting.
Propriety erects a wall around
The tender, easily offended sex.
Where rules morality, there they rule also,
Where impudence controls, they count for nothing.   1020
And if you make inquiry of both sexes:
Men strive for freedom, women for decorum.
TASSO: You term us coarse, unruly, feelingless?
PRINCESS: Not that. But you strive for far-off possessions,
And all your striving must be violent.
You make bold to act for eternity,
Whereas we only want to own a close

And limited estate upon this earth,
And want it to endure for us steadfastly.
Of no man's heart can we be sure, no matter   1030
How warmly it surrendered once to us.
Beauty, which you seem to esteem alone,
Is transitory. What remains has no
More charm, and what has no more charm, is dead.
If there were men who prized a female heart
And who could realize just what a gracious
Treasure of fidelity and love
Can be contained within a woman's breast;
If memory of uniquely lovely hours
Would vividly remain within your souls,   1040
If your glance, otherwise so penetrating,
Could also penetrate the veil that age
Or illness casts upon us; if possession
Which is supposed to give tranquillity
Did not make you lust for another's goods;
A splendid day would have appeared for us,
Then we would celebrate our golden age.
TASSO: You speak words which rouse powerfully within
My bosom cares that were half lulled asleep.
PRINCESS: What do you mean? Speak frankly with me, Tasso. 1050
TASSO: I often heard it said, and recently
Have heard it said again, and had I not
Heard, I would still have thought it: noble princes
Are suing for your hand! And what we must
Expect, we fear and we could utterly
Despair. For you will leave us, it is natural.
How we will bear it, though, I do not know.
PRINCESS: Have no fears for the present moment. I
Might almost say: have no fears whatsoever.
Here I am glad to be and glad to stay;   1060
I still know no engagement that would tempt me.
And if you want so much to keep me, show
Me so by harmony and make yourself

A happy life, and through you, one for me.
TASSO: O teach me how to do the possible!
 To you are dedicated all my days.
 When my heart is unfolded to praise you,
 To give you thanks, then only do I feel
 The purest happiness that man can know;
 Divinest things I learned through you alone.   1070
 Thus earthly gods from other humans are
 Distinguished, just as high fate is distinguished
 From the advice and will of even those
 Men who are most astute. So much they let
 Pass by unnoticed as light wavelets rippling
 Before their feet, when we see mighty wave
 On mighty wave; they do not hear the storm
 That rages all around and overthrows us;
 They barely hear our plea for help and let
 The air be filled with sighs and lamentation,   1080
 As we do with poor children of small mind.
 You often have, O godlike one, had patience
 With me, and like the sun your glance has dried
 The dew that welled from underneath my eyelids.
PRINCESS: It is entirely proper women should
 Treat you in friendly fashion, for your poem
 Glorifies the sex in many ways.
 Gentle or brave, you have consistently
 Presented them as lovable and noble,
 And though Armida does appear as hateful,   1090
 Her charm and love conciliate us quickly.
TASSO: Whatever things reecho in my poem,
 I owe them all to one, to one alone.
 No unclear, immaterial image hovers
 Before my brow, now dazzlingly approaching
 My soul and now retreating. I have seen
 It with my very eyes, the archetype
 Of every virtue and of every beauty.
 What I have copied from it will endure:

Heroic love of Tancred for Chlorinda,   1100
Erminia's quiet faithfulness unnoticed,
Sophronia's greatness and Olinda's pain,
These are not shadows by illusion bred;
I know they are eternal, for they *are*.
And what has any better right to last
For centuries and have prolonged effect
More than the secret of a noble love
Confided modestly to lovely song?

PRINCESS: Shall I tell you another excellence
Which has been caught unnoticed by this poem?   1110
It lures us on and on; we listen and
We listen, and we think we understand;
And what we understand we cannot blame;
And thus this poem finally wins us over.

TASSO: O what a heaven you disclose for me,
My Princess! If this splendor does not blind me,
I see eternal happiness unhoped-for
Descending gloriously on golden rays.

PRINCESS: No further, Tasso! There are many things
Which we must seize upon with vehemence,   1120
But others can be ours through self-restraint
Alone and through renunciation. Such,
They say, is virtue, such, they say, is love,
Which is related to it. Mark this well.
                    [Exit.]

TASSO *(alone):*
Is it allowable to raise your eyes?
Do you dare look about? You are alone!
And did these columns hear what she pronounced?
And need you fear these silent witnesses
Of highest happiness? There now is rising
The sun of a new day of my existence,   1130
With which the former will not be compared.
Descending low the goddess swiftly lifts
The mortal up. What a new sphere reveals

Itself before my vision, what a realm!
How richly is the ardent wish rewarded!
I dreamed that I was near to highest bliss,
And *this* bliss is beyond all of my dreams.
Let one who was born blind conceive of light
And colors as he may; if the new day
Appears to him, it is as a new sense.   1140
Foresensing, heartened, staggering drunk with joy,
I enter on this path. You give me much,
You give as earth and heaven shower gifts
Upon us lavishly and with full hands,
And in return ask only what a gift
Like this entitles you to ask of me.
I must renounce, I must show self-restraint,
And thus deserve that you confide in me.
What have I ever done that she could choose me?
What must I do now to be worthy of her?   1150
She could confide in you, and hence you are.
Yes, Princess, to your words and to your gaze
Let my soul be forever consecrated!
Ask anything you will, for I am yours!
Let her send me to seek for toil and peril
And fame in foreign lands, or let her hand me
The golden lyre amid the tranquil grove,
Ordain me for repose and praise of her:
Hers am I; forming me she shall possess me.
For *her* my heart has hoarded every treasure.   1160
O had capacity a thousand-fold
Been given me by a god, I scarcely could
Express my word-transcending adoration.
The painter's brush, the poet's lips, the sweetest
That on the early honey ever fed,
These I could wish to have. No, Tasso shall
Henceforth not stray in solitude and moody
And weak among the trees and human beings!
He is no more alone, he is with *you*.

O if the noblest of all feats would here 1170
Present itself before me visibly
Ringed round with grisly peril! I would throw
Myself upon it, gladly risk the life
That I now have from her hands — I would challenge
The finest human beings as my friends
To come with noble forces and perform
Impossibilities upon her beck
And call. Rash man, why did your mouth not hold
Back what you felt till you could lay yourself
Yet far more worthily before her feet? 1180
That was your purpose and your wiser wish.
But be it so! It is far finer to
Receive a gift like this unmerited
Than half and half to fancy that one might
Have had a right to ask for it. Look cheerily!
It is so great, so vast, what lies before you,
And hopeful youth entices you again
Into a radiant and unknown future.
— Swell high, my heart! — Climate of happiness,
Accord your favor to this plant for once! 1190
It strives toward heaven, and a thousand branches
Grow forth from it, unfolding into blossoms.
May it bear fruit, and O may it bear joy!
And may a dear hand pluck the golden apples
Off from its fresh and richly laden boughs!
                    [Enter Antonio.]
Welcome to you whom I behold now, as
It were, for the first time. No man was ever
More admirably announced to me. Hence, welcome!
I know you now and I know your full worth;
I offer heart and hand unhesitating 1200
And hope that you will not disdain me either.
ANTONIO: Fair gifts you offer me, and generously,
    I recognize their value as I should,
    Hence let me hesitate before I take them.

I do not know yet whether I in turn
Can offer you the same. I should not like
To seem in over-haste nor seem ungrateful;
Let me be prudent and concerned for both.

TASSO: Who will blame prudence? Every step in life
Reveals how indispensable it is.   1210
But it is finer when the soul informs us
Where we have no need of its circumspection.

ANTONIO: On that score let each man ask his own heart,
For he must pay for his mistake himself.

TASSO: So be it, then. I have performed my duty.
I have revered the Princess's command,
Who wants to see us friends, and have presented
Myself to you. Hold back, Antonio, I could not,
But I shall surely not impose myself.
Time and acquaintance will perhaps bring you   1220
To ask more warmly for the gift which you
Now coldly put aside and almost scorn.

ANTONIO: A self-restrained man often is termed cold
By those who think themselves more warm than others
Because a fleeting heat comes over them.

TASSO: You censure what I censure, what I shun.
I too am capable, young as I am,
Of putting permanency over fervor.

ANTONIO: Most wisely so! Be always of that mind.

TASSO: You are entitled to advise me and   1230
To warn me, for you have Experience at
Your side as proven and long-standing friend.
Still, credit that a quiet heart does harken
To every day's and every hour's warning
And practices in secret all the virtues
Your strictness thinks to teach as something new.

ANTONIO: It is agreeable to be concerned
With one's own self, if that but serve a purpose.
By introspection no man can discover
His inmost heart; by his own measure he   1240

Will judge himself too small, or else, alas,
Too great. Man knows himself through man alone
And only life can teach him what he is.

TASSO: I hear you with approval and respect.

ANTONIO: And yet at these words you are doubtless thinking
Something quite different from what I intend.

TASSO: In this way we will not come any nearer.
It is not sensible, it profits nothing
To misjudge any man deliberately,
Let him be who he may. I hardly needed   1250
The Princess's command, I quickly knew you:
I realize you wish and do the good.
Your own fate leaves you wholly unconcerned,
You think of others, give support to others,
And on the lightly changeful wave of life
Retain a steadfast heart. So I perceive you.
What would I be if I did not approach you
And did not eagerly seek to acquire
A portion of the treasure you are hoarding?
I know you won't regret it if you open   1260
Your heart, I know that you will be my friend
When once you know me, and I long have needed
Just such a friend. I feel my inexperience
And youth no cause for shame. About my head
The future's golden cloud still gently hovers.
O take me, noble man, unto your bosom
And consecrate me, rash and inexperienced,
Unto the temperate usages of life.

ANTONIO: All in a single minute you ask for
What time alone can grant with careful thought.   1270

TASSO: Within a single minute love will grant
What effort barely gains in length of time.
I do not ask this of you, I demand it.
I call upon you in that virtue's name
That vies in the allying of good men.
And shall I name a further name to you?

The Princess hopes for it, *she* wishes it —
Eleonore — she wants to bring me
To you and you to me. O let us meet
Her wish! Let us both go before that goddess   1280
And offer her our service, our whole souls,
United, to perform the utmost for her.
Once again! — Here is my hand! Clasp it!
Do not step back, refuse yourself no longer,
O noble man, and grant me the delight,
The best good human beings know, of yielding,
Without reserve, in trust, up to a better.

ANTONIO: You go with all sails crowded. It would seem
You are accustomed to win out, to find
The roads smooth everywhere and gates wide open.   1290
I willingly allow you every worth
And every lucky chance; but I see only
Too clearly we still stand too far apart.

TASSO: In years, in tested merit, that may be;
In courage and in will I yield to none.

ANTONIO: It is not will that coaxes high feats up,
And courage will imagine shorter ways.
A man who has achieved his goal is crowned;
A worthy one will often lack a crown.
There are, however, facile crowns, and there   1300
Are crowns of very different sorts. Sometimes
They can be comfortably achieved on strolls.

TASSO: What godhead freely grants to one and sternly
Refuses to another, such a prize
Will not be every man's to wish and will.

ANTONIO: Give Luck the credit over other gods
And I will listen, for his choice is blind.

TASSO: But Justice also wears a blindfold and
Has closed eyes in the face of all delusion.

ANTONIO: A lucky man may well extol Good Luck,   1310
And for the service may impute to him
A hundred eyes, shrewd choice, and strict discernment,

Call it Minerva, call it what he will,
Accept a gracious gift as a reward,
And take chance trimmings for well won adornment.

TASSO: You need not speak more plainly. This is quite enough!
I now see deep into your heart and know
You for a lifetime. O would that my Princess
Also knew you this way! Do not waste
The arrows of your eyes and of your tongue!   1320
You aim them futilely against the wreath,
The never-fading wreath upon my head.
First be so great as not begrudge me it
And then perhaps you may contest me for it.
I deem it sacred, a supreme possession.
Show me the man who has achieved the thing
That I am striving for, show me the hero
Of whom the stories merely told the tale,
Show me the poet who may be compared
With Homer and with Vergil, yes, and what   1330
Goes further still, show me the man who ever
Deserved with triple merit that reward
And yet was three times more than I ashamed
Of that fair crown, — then you will see me on
My knees before the god who so endowed me,
Nor would I rise until that god transferred
That mark of honor from my head to his.

ANTONIO: Till then, admittedly, you merit it.

TASSO: Appraise my worth: I will not shrink from that.
But I have not deserved contempt. The crown   1340
That my Prince deemed me worthy of and which
My Princess' hand entwined for me shall not
Be cast in doubt by sneers from anyone!

ANTONIO: Your high tone and swift heat do not beseem you
With me, and are not seemly in this place.

TASSO: What you presumed here may beseem me also.
Has truth perhaps been banished from this place?
Is the free mind imprisoned in the palace?

Must noble men endure oppression here?
Highness is here, I fancy, in its proper place,   1350
The highness of the soul! May it not joy
In presence of the great ones of this earth?
It may and shall. We come close to a Prince
By noble blood alone, ours from our forefathers,
But why not by the mind that Nature granted
Not great to every man, as she could not
Give every man a line of noble ancestors.
Smallness alone should feel uneasy here,
And envy, that appears to its own shame,
Just as no spider's filthy web may be   1360
Allowed to cling upon these marble walls.

ANTONIO: You prove me right yourself in spurning you!
    And so the over-hasty boy would get
    By force the grown man's confidence and friendship?
    Ill-bred as you are, do you think you're good?

TASSO: Far rather what you choose to term ill-bred
    Than what I could not help but term ignoble.

ANTONIO: You still are young enough that proper training
    Can teach you something of a better way.

TASSO: Not young enough to bow in front of idols;   1370
    To brave defiance with defiance, old
    Enough.

ANTONIO: Where lip and lyre decide the contest
    You do come off the hero and the victor.

TASSO: It would be rash to boast about my fists;
    They have done nothing, but I trust in them.

ANTONIO: You reckon on forbearance, which has only
    Spoiled you too much in arrogant good fortune.

TASSO: That I am grown to manhood, I now feel.
    You are the last with whom I should have liked
    To try the hazard of a pass with weapons,   1380
    But you rake fire on top of fire until
    My inmost marrow scorches and the painful
    Lust for revenge seethes foaming in my breast.

So if you are the man you boast of, face me.

ANTONIO: You know as little who, as where, you are.

TASSO: No sanctuary bids us bear abuse.
    You blaspheme and you desecrate this place,
    Not I, who offered you my confidence,
    Respect, and love, the finest offerings.
    Your spirit has defiled this paradise   1390
    And your words now defile this stainless room,
    Not my heart's surge of passion which now rages
    At suffering the slightest spot of soilure.

ANTONIO: What lofty spirit in that pent-up bosom!

TASSO: Here is still room to give that bosom vent.

ANTONIO: The rabble also vent their hearts with words.

TASSO: If you're a nobleman as I am, show it.

ANTONIO: Such am I, but I know, too, where I am.

TASSO: Come down then where our weapons may avail.

ANTONIO: You should not challenge, and I will not come.   1400

TASSO: Such obstacles are welcome to a coward.

ANTONIO: The coward threatens only where he's safe.

TASSO: With joy I can dispense with that protection.

ANTONIO: You compromise yourself, this place you cannot.

TASSO: The place forgive me for enduring this!
                    (He draws his sword.)
    Draw or come after, if I am not to
    Despise you, as I hate you, evermore!
                    [Enter Alfonso.]

ALFONSO: In what contention do I chance upon you?

ANTONIO: You find me standing calmly, O my Prince,
    Before a man whom rage has seized upon.   1410

TASSO: Ah, I adore you as a deity for
    Restraining me with just one glance of warning.

ALFONSO: Recount, Antonio, Tasso, and inform me
    How did dissension get into my house?
    How did it seize upon you, carrying off
    In frenzy sane men from the path of proper
    Behavior and of laws? I am astonished.

TASSO: I do not think that you quite know us both.
    This man, renowned as sensible and upright,
    Has treated me maliciously and rudely   1420
    Like an ill-bred and an ignoble man.
    I had approached him trustfully, but he
    Thrust me away; I in persistent love
    Pressed on, and ever more, more bitterly
    He did not rest till he had turned the purest
    Drop of blood in me to gall. Forgive me!
    You found me like a madman here. This man
    Is all to blame if I incurred a guilt.
    He was the one who fiercely fanned the fire
    That seized me and offended me and him.   1430
ANTONIO: His high poetic flight swept him away!
    You did, O Prince, address me first and asked
    Of me. Then let me be permitted to
    Speak second after this rash talker now.
TASSO: O yes! Relate, relate it word for word!
    And if you can put every syllable
    And every look before this judge, just dare!
    Disgrace yourself now for a second time
    And testify against yourself! And I
    Will not deny one breath or pulse-beat of it.   1440
ANTONIO: If you have any more to say, then say it.
    If not, be still and do not interrupt me.
    Did I, my Prince, or did this hothead here
    Begin the quarrel? Which one was it who
    Was in the wrong? That is an ample question
    Which for the moment must wait in abeyance.
TASSO: What? I should think that that was the first question,
    Which one of us is right and which is wrong.
ANTONIO: Not just the way the unrestricted mind
    May fancy it.
ALFONSO: Antonio!
ANTONIO: Gracious Lord,   1450
    I honor your behest, but keep him quiet.

Once I have spoken, he can talk again.
You will decide. Thus I will merely say:
I cannot argue with him, I can neither
Accuse him, nor defend myself, nor offer
Myself to give him satisfaction now.
For as he stands, he is not a free man.
A heavy law holds sway above him, which
Your favor at the most can mitigate.
He made threats to me here, he challenged me,   1460
He hardly hid his naked sword from you,
And had you, Lord, not intervened between us,
I too would stand here now as one disloyal,
Accessory to guilt, and shamed before you.

ALFONSO *(to Tasso):*
    You have not acted well.

TASSO: My own heart, Lord,
Acquits me; yours will surely do the same.
Yes, it is true, I made threats, challenged him,
And drew. But how insidiously his tongue
Offended me with well selected words,
How sharp and swift his fang injected its   1470
Fine venom in my blood, how he enflamed
The fever more and more, — you can't imagine!
Calmly, coldly, he kept at me, drove
Me to the highest pitch. O you don't know
Him, you don't know him, you will never know him!
I warmly offered him the finest friendship
And he threw my gift down before my feet.
Had my soul not flamed up with passion, it
Would be eternally unworthy of
Your favor and your service. If I did   1480
Forget the law and this place here, forgive me.
On no spot can I ever be abject,
On no spot can I bear humiliation.
If this heart ever, be it where it may,
Fails you and fails itself, then cast me out

And never let me see your face again.
ANTONIO: How easily this youth bears heavy burdens
  And shakes off faults like dust out of a garment!
  It would be quite amazing, were the magic power
  Of poetry not so well known, that loves   1490
  So well to sport with the impossible.
  I have my doubts, my Prince, that you and all
  Your followers will look upon this deed
  As being quite so insignificant.
  For majesty extends its high protection
  To every man that comes to it as to
  A goddess and to its inviolate
  Abode. As at the altar steps, all passion
  Will hold itself in check upon her threshold.
  There no sword gleams, no threatening word is uttered,   1500
  Offense itself demands no vengeance there.
  Broad fields provide sufficient open space
  For fury and implacability.
  No coward threatens there, no man takes flight.
  These walls your fathers founded here upon
  Security, and for their dignity
  Made strong a sanctuary, solemnly
  Maintaining peace by heavy penalties.
  There prison, death, and exile overtook
  The guilty; neither did regard for persons   1510
  Or clemency restrain the arm of justice.
  The wicked man himself was terror-stricken.
  Now after long and splendid peace we see
  Raw fury staggering back again in frenzy
  Into the jurisdiction of right conduct.
  Judge, Lord, and punish! Who can walk within
  Set limits of his duty if the law
  And if his Prince's power does not shield him?
ALFONSO: More than you both have said or ever could say
  My own impartial mind gives me to hear.   1520
  You would have done your duty vastly better

If I did not have to pronounce this judgment.
For right and wrong are close-related here.
If from Antonio you sustained offense,
Then he must give you satisfaction in
Some way or other, as you will demand.
I would prefer it if you chose me for
The arbitration. Meanwhile, your crime, Tasso,
Makes you a prisoner. As I forgive you,
I will alleviate the law for your sake.   1530
Leave us, Tasso. Stay in your own room,
Your own sole guard and by yourself alone.

TASSO: Is this, O Prince, your sentence as a judge?

ANTONIO: Do you not recognize a father's mildness?

TASSO *(to Antonio):*

To you I have no more to at say present.

(to Alfonso)

O Prince, your solemn sentence gives me over,
A free man, to imprisonment. So be it!
You deem it just. Your sacred word obeying,
I bid my heart be still to deepest depths.
This is so new to me that I almost   1540
Do not know you, myself, or this fair place.
But this man I know well — I will obey,
Although I still could say a lot of things,
And ought to say them, too. My lips fall silent.
Was there a crime? It seems at least that I
Am being looked on as a criminal.
Speak my heart as it may, I am a captive.

ALFONSO: You make it graver, Tasso, than I do.

TASSO: It is incomprehensible to me.

O not incomprehensible exactly,   1550
I am no child. I almost think I must
Have grasped it. Sudden light does dawn on me
But in an instant closes up again.
I hear my sentence only, and I bow.
There are too many useless words already!

Acquire henceforth the habit of obeying.
You, feeble man, forgot where you were standing,
The gods' hall seemed to stand on equal earth
With you, and now the steep fall overwhelms you.
Obey with a good will, for it befits   1560
A man to do with good will what is painful.
First take this sword that you had given me
When I went with the Cardinal to France.
I wore it with no fame, nor yet with shame,
Not even here today. This hopeful gift
I yield up with a heart profoundly moved.
ALFONSO: You do not feel how I am minded toward you.
TASSO: Obedience is my lot, and not to think!
Unfortunately a splendid gift's refusal
Is what my destiny requires of me.   1570
Nor does a crown befit a captive: I
Remove the mark of honor from my head
Myself, that I thought given for all time.
That finest fortune was vouchsafed too early
And, as if I had overreached myself,
Is taken from me all too soon.
You take yourself what no one could take from you,
And what no god will give a second time.
We human beings have most wondrous trials;
We could not bear it, were it not that Nature   1580
Endowed us with a blessed levity.
Distress invites us to play recklessly
And coolly with possessions beyond price,
And willingly we open up our hands
For such a thing to slip past all recall.
There is a tear united with this kiss,
Devoting you to transitoriness.
It is permissible, this mark of weakness.
Who would not weep when an immortal thing
Itself is not safe from annihilation?   1590
Come, join this sword, which had no part, alas,

In winning you, and, twined about it, rest,
As on the coffin of the brave, upon
The tomb of my good fortune and my hope.
I willingly lay both before your feet,
For who is well armed if you are in anger,
And who adorned, Lord, if you fail to note him?
I go, a captive, to await my judgment.
          (*At the Prince's sign, a page picks up the*
          sword and wreath and carries them away.)
ANTONIO: Where is the boy's wild raving taking him?
    In what hues does he paint his fate and merits?   1600
    Restricted, inexperienced, youth considers
    Itself as a unique and elect being
    To whom all is allowed above all others.
    Let him feel punished; punishment is good
    For youth, and the adult will thank us for it.
ALFONSO: Punished he is; I only fear: too much.
ANTONIO: If you wish to deal leniently with him,
    Then give him back, O Prince, his liberty
    And let the sword then settle our dispute.
ALFONSO: If opinion so requires, that may be done.   1610
    But tell me, how did you provoke his anger?
ANTONIO: I scarcely can say how it came about.
    I may perhaps have hurt his human feelings,
    But as a nobleman I gave him no
    Offense, and at the height of anger no
    Improper word escaped his lips.
ALFONSO: So seemed
    Your quarrel to me, and what I thought at once
    Is all the more confirmed by what you say.
    When grown men quarrel, one may justly hold
    The shrewder one responsible. You ought   1620
    Not to be angry with him; guiding him
    Would more become you. But there still is time.
    This is no case that would require a duel.
    As long as peace remains to me, I want

Just so long to enjoy it in my house.
Restore a calm, you can do so with ease.
Lenore Sanvitale will first seek
With gentle lips to sooth his agitation.
Then go to him, and in my name restore
His total liberty to him and gain   1630
His confidence with honest, noble words.
Perform this just as soon as possible.
You will talk to him like a friend and father.
I want peace made before we go away,
And nothing is impossible to you
When once you will. Best we delay an hour,
Then let the ladies gently finish up
What you began; when we ourselves get back,
They will have wiped out every trace of this
Abrupt impression. It appears, Antonio,   1640
That you will not get out of practice. You
Have barely finished with one task, when back
You come and straightway get yourself another.
I trust you will succeed in this one also.
ANTONIO: I am abashed, and in your words I see
My guilt as in the clearest mirror. With
Alacrity a man obeys a master
Who can persuade us as he gives commands.   (1648)

ACT III

THE PRINCESS *(alone):* Where does Eleonore stay? Concern
  More painfully with every moment stirs   1650
  My deepest heart. I scarcely know what happened,
  I scarcely know which one if them is guilty.
  If she would only come! I should not like
  To speak yet with my brother or Antonio
  Until I am more calm, till I have heard
  How things now stand and what may come to be.
               [Enter Leonore.]
  What news do you bring, Leonore? Tell me,
  How do things stand now with our friend? What happened?
LEONORE: I could not learn more than we know already.
  They harshly clashed, and Tasso drew his sword,   1660
  Your brother parted them. It seems, however,
  That it was Tasso who began the quarrel.
  Antonio walks about conversing with
  His Prince, while Tasso on the other hand
  Remains alone and banished in his room.
PRINCESS: Antonio provoked him certainly
  And coldly gave the high-strung youth offense.
LEONORE: I have the same opinion, for there was
  A cloud upon his brow when he arrived.
PRINCESS: Alas, that we fail so completely to   1670
  Observe the pure, mute signal of the heart!
  A god speaks very softly in our bosoms,
  Softly and audibly, and shows us what
  We should accept and what we should avoid.
  Antonio seemed to me this morning much
  More gruff, withdrawn into himself, than ever.

51

When Tasso went up to him then, my mind
Gave me a warning. Just observe the outer
Appearance of the two, in face, in voice,
In look, in gait. All points in opposition;   1680
They cannot ever give each other love.
But that dissembler, Hope, persuaded me
And whispered: Both of them are rational men,
Both noble, erudite, and both your friends.
What bond is surer than that of good men?
I urged the youth and he agreed completely;
How warm and fine his acquiescence was!
O had I only spoken with Antonio!
I hesitated; there was little time,
I shrank from recommending urgently   1690
The youth to him in the first words I spoke;
I trusted to good manners and politeness,
In social usage which is interposed
So smoothly even between enemies,
And from the tested man had no fear of
A rash youth's over-haste. But it is done.
The evil was far off, now it is here.
O give me counsel! What is to be done?
LEONORE: You feel yourself how difficult it is
To counsel after what you tell me. Here   1700
Is no like-minded men's misunderstanding;
Words could set that aright, or weapons could,
If needs be, easily and happily.
But these are two men, as I long have felt,
Who must be enemies because great Nature
Did not form one man from the two of them.
And if they were shrewd for their own advantage,
They would ally themselves as friends together.
Then they would stand as one man and would walk
Along through life with joy and might and fortune.   1710
I had so hoped, but now I see, in vain.
Today's dissension, be it as it may,

Can be composed, but that gives no assurance
For future times, not even for tomorrow.
It would be best for Tasso, I should think,
To travel for a time away from here.
Why, he could go to Rome, and Florence too;
There in a few weeks I could meet him and
Could work upon his spirits as a friend.
Meanwhile, Antonio, who has become   1720
So alien to us, you would be bringing
Closer to you and to your friends once more.
In that way time, that does so much, perhaps
Might grant what now seems quite impossible.
PRINCESS: You want the pleasure for yourself, my friend,
    While I must do without. Is that quite nice?
LEONORE: You will not do without, except for what
    You could not now enjoy in any case.
PRINCESS: Am I to send a friend away so calmly?
LEONORE: Retain him, whom you only seem to banish.   1730
PRINCESS: My brother will not willingly release him.
LEONORE: When he sees it as we do, he will yield.
PRINCESS: Condemning oneself in a friend is hard.
LEONORE: Yet you will save your friend thus in yourself.
PRINCESS: I do not cast my vote for it to happen.
LEONORE: Then look for greater evil yet to come.
PRINCESS: You pain me, while unsure if you are helping.
LEONORE: We soon shall learn which one of us is wrong.
PRINCESS: And if it is to be, ask me no longer.
LEONORE: One who can make decisions, conquers sorrow.   1740
PRINCESS: I cannot quite decide, but be it so
    If he is not to be away for long —
    Let us be watchful for him, Leonore,
    That he not suffer want in times to come
    And that the Duke may willingly advance
    His stipend to him even while abroad.
    Talk with Antonio, for with my brother
    He has much influence and will not hold

This quarrel against us or against our friend.

LEONORE: One word from you would, Princess, have more   1750
                                         weight.

PRINCESS: I am not able, as you know, my friend,
    To ask things for myself and for my own
    The way my sister of Urbino can.
    I live my life so quietly, and from
    My brother gratefully accept whatever
    He can and wishes to provide me with.
    I used once to reproach myself for this,
    But I have overcome that feeling now.
    A friend of mine would often scold me for it.
    "You are unselfish," she would say to me,   1760
    "And that is splendid; but you are so much so
    That you can have no just perception of
    Your friends' requirements either." I admit it
    And must therefore put up with that reproach.
    Hence I am all the better pleased that I
    Now really can be of use to our friend.
    I do receive my mother's legacy,
    And I will gladly help toward his support.

LEONORE: And I too find myself in a position,
    O Princess, where I can help as a friend.   1770
    He does not manage well, and where he lacks,
    I will be able to assist him nicely.

PRINCESS: Take him away, then, and if I must do
    Without him, you shall have first claim on him.
    I realize it will be best that way.
    But must I praise this sorrow once again
    As good and wholesome? That was my fate ever
    From childhood, I am used to it by now.
    But happiness is no more than half lost
    If we did not count its possession certain.   1780

LFONORE: Deserving as you are, I hope to see
    You happy.

PRINCESS: Happy? O Eleonore!

Who ever is quite happy? — I might term
My brother so, for his great heart endures
His destiny with ever equal courage.
But what he merits, never has been his.
And is my sister of Urbino happy?
That lovely woman, great and noble heart!
She bears no children to her younger husband
And he esteems her and does not hold it   1790
Against her, but no joy dwells in their house.
What was the good of all our mother's wisdom,
Her learning of all kinds, and her great mind?
Could it protect her from mistakes of others?
They parted us from her; now she is dead.
She did not leave us children with the comfort
That she died reconciled unto her God.

LEONORE: O do not look at what all persons lack,
    Consider what remains for each! What, Princess,
    Does not remain for you?

PRINCESS: Remain for me?   1800
    Patience, Eleonore! I could practice that
    From childhood up. While sister, brother, friends
    Gregariously had joy in games and parties,
    My illness kept me shut within my room,
    And in the company of many ailments
    I early had to learn to do without.
    One thing there was that charmed my solitude,
    The joy of song; I used to entertain
    Myself myself, I lulled my pain, my yearning,
    My every wish, to sleep with gentle tones.   1810
    Grief often turned to pleasure then, and even
    The sense of sadness turned to harmony.
    That happiness was not allowed me long,
    The doctor took that too away; his strict
    Command bade me be still. I was to live,
    To suffer, and to renounce the least small comfort.

LEONORE: So many friends came in to see you, and

You now are well and take delight in life.

PRINCESS: Yes, I am well, which means I am not ill;
And I have many friends whose faithfulness   1820
Does make me glad. I also had a friend —

LEONORE: You have him still.

PRINCESS: But I shall lose him soon.
The moment when I first caught sight of him
Meant much to me. I hardly had recovered
From many sufferings, and pain and illness
Had only just departed; timidly
I looked at life again, joyed in the daylight
Again, and in my brother and my sister,
And with new strength inhaled sweet hope's pure fragrance.
I ventured to look further forward into   1830
Life's vistas, and out of the further distance
Came forms of friends approaching me. And then,
Eleonore, came my sister and presented
This youth to me; he came led by her hand,
And, to confess quite frankly, my soul seized
Upon him and will hold him fast forever.

LEONORE: Have no regrets on that score, O my Princess!
To recognize nobility is gain,
A gain that never can be wrested from us.

PRINCESS: Things beautiful and excellent are to be feared,   1840
As flame is, that is of such splendid use
So long as it burns only on your hearth,
So long as it shines for you from a torch,
How lovely! Who can or who wants to do
Without it? Once it eats abroad unguarded,
How wretched it can make us! Leave me now.
I have been garrulous and should conceal
Even from you how weak I am, and ill.

LEONORE: The illness of the spirit is relieved
Most easily by grieving and confiding.   1850

PRINCESS: I shall be healed soon if confiding heals:
To you I give full confidence and pure.

Alas, my friend, I have made up my mind:
Let him depart. But I already feel
The long protracted suffering of those days when
I am deprived of what gave me delight.
The sun no longer will lift from my eyelids
His beautiful, transfigured dream-impression;
The hope of seeing him no more will fill
My scarce awakened mind with joyous yearning;   1860
My first glance down into our gardens will
Seek him in vain amid the dewy shadows.
How pleasingly the wish was gratified
To be with him on every cheerful evening!
How our companionship increased the wish
To know and understand each other better.
Each day our spirits tuned themselves more truly
In pure and ever purer harmonies.
But what a twilight now descends before me!
The sun's resplendency, the happy feeling   1870
Of lofty day, the thousandfold world's bright
And radiant presence are all empty and
Veiled deep within the mist that is around me.
Before, each day was a whole life to me;
Foreboding's self was still, and care was silent,
And under joyous sail, the river bore us
Along on lightest waves without a rudder.
Now terrors of the future overwhelm
My heart in stealth amid the dismal present.
LEONORE: The future will return your friends to you   1880
And bring new joy and happiness as well.
PRINCESS: Whatever I possess I like to keep.
Change brings diversion but does little good.
In youthful yearning I have never reached
With greed into strange persons' urns of fate
To seize perchance upon some object for
My own requiring, inexperienced heart.
I had to honor him, therefore I loved him;

I had to love him, for with him my life
Became a life such as I never knew.   1890
I told myself at first: Withdraw from him!
I yielded, yielded, and came ever closer,
So sweetly lured and yet so harshly punished.
A pure and true possession now escapes me;
For joy and happiness an evil spirit
Now gives my longing corresponding sorrows.

LEONORE: If a friend's words can give no consolation,
The quiet power of the lovely world
And better times will unperceived restore you.

PRINCESS: The world indeed is beautiful! Across   1900
Its breadth so much of good moves back and forth.
Alas, that it forever seems to move
By just one step away from us
And lure our fearful yearning on through life,
Step after step, up to our very graves!
It is so rarely human beings find
What seemed to have been theirs by destiny,
So rarely that they ever can retain
What once their hands successfully have seized on!
What first submitted to us, wrenches free   1910
And we relinquish what so avidly
We clutched. There is a happiness; we know
It not, or knowing, know not how to prize it.

[Exit.]

LEONORE *(alone):* How sad I feel for that fine, noble heart!
How sad the lot that now falls to Her Highness!
She loses — and do you think you will gain?
Is it so needful that he go away?
Or do you make it needful, to obtain
The heart and talents for yourself which up
To now you have shared with another — shared   1920
Unequally? Is acting thus quite honest?
Are you not rich enough? What do you lack for?
Husband and son, possessions, rank and beauty,

All these you have, and still you want him too
With all the rest? Are you in love with him?
What reason else is there why you can't do
Without him? To yourself you can confess it —
How charming it is to behold oneself
Mirrored in his fine mind! Is happiness
Not doubly great and splendid when his song   1930
Exalts and carries us as if on clouds?
Then only are you enviable! You *are,*
Not merely *have,* the thing that many wish for —
And everyone knows and sees the thing you have!
Your fatherland names you and looks at you,
That is the pinnacle of happiness.
Must *Laura* be the one and only name
That is to sound upon all tender lips?
Did only Petrarch have the right to raise
An unknown beauty up to goddesshood?   1940
Where is there any man to be compared
With my friend? As the world reveres him now,
So aftertimes will reverence him as well.
How wonderful it is to have him at
One's side amid the splendor of this life
And with light step move with him toward the future!
No power then will time or old age have
Upon you, nor brash reputation
That drives approval's wave this way and that.
Things transitory his song will preserve.   1950
You are still beautiful, still happy, even
Though long swept onward by the round of things.
And you must have him, from her you take nothing,
For her affection for the worthy man
Is similar to all her other passions.
They shed a scanty gleam like quiet moonlight
Upon the traveler's pathway in the night.
They give no warmth and cast no pleasure round
About, nor joy of life. She will be glad

Once she knows he is gone, knows he is happy,   1960
Just as she joyed in seeing him each day.
Besides, I will not banish myself with
My friend either from her or from this court,
I will come back, and bring him back as well.
So let it be! — Here comes our rude friend now.
We shall find out if we can tame him down.
                [Enter Antonio.]
You bring us war instead of peace; it seems
As if you came from camp or from a battle
Where violence prevails and force decides,
And not from Rome, where solemn sagacity   1970
Uplifts its hands in blessing and beholds
Before its feet a world that gladly harkens.
ANTONIO: That blame I must acknowledge, lovely friend,
But my excuse lies no great distance off.
There is a peril in behaving wisely
And moderately too long a time. There lurks
An evil genius at your side who will
From time to time demand a sacrifice
By dint of force. Unfortunately this time
I gave it to him at my friends' expense.   1980
LEONORE: You have so long directed efforts toward
Strange people and been guided by their minds,
That, now you see your friends again, you quite
Mistake them and dispute as if with strangers.
ANTONIO: There lies the danger, my beloved friend!
With strangers one will pull himself together,
Be on his guard, and in their favor seek
His purpose, so that they may be of use.
But with one's friends one lets himself go freely,
One rests upon their love, permits himself   1990
Caprices, passion has a more untamed
Effect, and thereby we offend first off
The very ones we love most tenderly.
LEONORE: In this reposeful observation I find you

Once more, dear friend, completely, and rejoice.
ANTONIO: Yes, I am vexed — and willingly confess it —
  For having strayed so out of bounds today.
  Grant me, however, when an honest man
  With brow all hot comes home from sour labor,
  And thinks late in the evening he will rest   2000
  In wished-for shade before his new exertions,
  And finds the shady place all taken up
  Then by an idler, shall he also not
  Feel something human stir inside his bosom?
LEONORE: If he is truly human he will share
  The shady spot quite gladly with a man
  Who sweetens his repose and makes work easy
  By conversation and by lovely tones.
  The tree is broad, my friend, that gives the shade,
  And neither needs to drive the other out.   2010
ANTONIO: O let us not, Eleonore, play
  Here back and forth thus with a metaphor.
  In this world there are many things that one
  Will grant another and will gladly share.
  But there is one thing precious which one will
  Grant gladly to the high-deserving only,
  Another which with good will one will never
  Share even with one who deserves the utmost —
  And if you ask what these two treasures are,
  They are the laurel leaf and women's favor.   2020
LEONORE: Did that wreath on our young man's head offend
  The earnest-minded man? But you yourself
  Could not have found a more discreet reward
  For all his work and for his splendid poem.
  A merit that stands outside of this earth,
  That hovers in the air, and flutters only
  In tones and in light images around
  Our minds, can only be rewarded with
  A pretty image and a lovely symbol.
  And if he barely touches earth himself,   2030

His head is barely touched by that supreme
Award. That gift is but a sterile branch
Presented to him by admirers' sterile
Affection, so they may most easily
Discharge a debt. You hardly will begrudge
The golden halo on the bald head in
A martyr's picture; and the laurel crown,
Wherever you may find it, certainly
Is more a sign of suffering than joy.

ANTONIO: Would your delightful lips be trying to   2040
Teach me contempt for this world's vanity?

LEONORE: I do not need to teach you how to prize
All things possessed at their just worth. And yet
It seems that wise men need from time to time,
As much as others, to have people show them
The things that they possess in their true light.
You, noble man, you will not make a claim
Upon a phantom of favor and honor.
The service wherewith you bind yourself to
Your Prince, wherewith you bind your friends to you,   2050
Is vital and effective; its reward
Must also be effective and alive.
Your laurel is your Prince's confidence,
Which rests as a beloved burden on
Your shoulders and is lightly borne; your fame
Consists of universal trust in you.

ANTONIO: But still of women's favor you say nothing:
You will not claim it is superfluous?

LEONORE: That all depends. You do not lack for it,
And you could sooner get along without it   2060
Than could that kindly man of whom you speak.
For tell me, would a woman be successful
If in her fashion she sought to care for you
And undertook to be concerned with you?
With you all is security and order;
You take care of yourself and others too;

You have what one would like to give you. He
Engages us in our own special field.
He lacks a thousand little things, which to
Procure a woman gladly bends her efforts.   2070
He likes to wear the finest linen, or
A silken garment with embroidery.
He likes to see himself in fine array;
Ignoble stuff that suits a lackey only
He cannot bear, and everything of his
Must be becoming, fine, and good, and noble.
And yet he has no skill in getting all
These things himself, or when he does possess them,
In keeping them; he always lacks for money,
For prudent care. He will leave one thing here,   2080
And leave another there, — he never comes
Back from a journey but that one third of
His things are missing, — then again his servant
Will steal from him. And so, Antonio,
One needs to take care of him all year long.

ANTONIO: And that care makes him dear and dearer still.
O happy youth, to have shortcomings reckoned
As virtues, be so handsomely allowed
To play the boy still while a man, be able
To boast about his lovely weaknesses!   2090
You would have to forgive me, my fair friend,
If I were to become a trifle bitter.
You don't tell all, — what he presumes, for instance,
And that he is more shrewd than people think.
He boasts two flames of love! ties and unties
The knots now one way, now another, and
By *such* arts wins *such* hearts! Would anyone
Believe it?

LEONORE: Good! That very fact will prove
That it is only friendship that impels us.
And even if we traded love for love,   2100
Would we not cheaply pay that splendid heart

That quite forgets itself and in devotion
Lives for its friends amid a lovely dream?
ANTONIO: Go on and spoil him, more and ever more,
    Allow his selfishness to pass for love,
    Offend all friends who dedicate themselves
    To you with loyal souls, pay that proud man
    Your voluntary tribute, and destroy
    The worthy circle of a common trust!
LEONORE: We are not quite so partial as you think,   2110
    We do admonish our young friend in many
    Cases; we want to educate him so
    He can enjoy himself more and give others
    More to enjoy. What is blameworthy in him
    Is not by any means obscured from us.
ANTONIO: Yet you praise many things that should be blamed.
    I long have known him, for he is so easy
    To know, and too proud to conceal himself.
    He sinks into himself as if the world
    Were all inside his heart and he were wholly   2120
    Sufficient to himself within his world,
    And all around him disappears for him.
    He drops it, lets it go, thrusts it away,
    And rests upon himself. — Then suddenly
    As an unnoticed spark ignites the mine,
    In joy, grief, whim, or anger, he explodes;
    Then he wants to grasp everything and hold it,
    Then must be done whatever he may fancy,
    Within a moment's space must come about
    What ought to be prepared through length of years,   2130
    Within a moment's space must be removed
    What effort scarcely could resolve in years.
    He asks from himself the impossible
    So that he may in turn ask it of others.
    His mind wants to assemble ultimates
    Of things together; scarcely one from millions
    Of human beings can succeed in that,

And he is not the man. He falls at last,
No wise improved, right back into himself.

LEONORE: He harms himself, he does no harm to others.   2140

ANTONIO: He does hurt other people all too much.
Can you deny that in the moment of
The passion that so swiftly seizes him
He will presume to blaspheme and abuse
The Prince, the Princess' self, or whomsoever?
Just for the moment, to be sure. However,
That moment will recur, for he controls
His mouth as little as he does his heart.

LEONORE: I should imagine, if he went away
From here for a brief time, it would be good   2150
For him and also profit others too.

ANTONIO: Perhaps; perhaps not. Right now it is not
To be considered; for I do not want
The burden of the error on my shoulders.
It might appear that I drove him away,
And I do not drive him away. For all
I care, he can stay at our court in peace.
And if he wishes to be reconciled
With me, if he can follow my advice,
Then we can get along quite tolerably.   2160

LEONORE: Then you hope to have influence upon
A spirit that you recently thought hopeless.

ANTONIO: We always hope, and it is better in
All things to hope than to despair. For who
Can calculate what all is possible?
He is dear to our Prince. He must stay with us.
And if we try in vain to educate him,
He will not be the only one we bear with.

LEONORE: I did not think you so impartial, so
Devoid of passion. Your mind swiftly changed.   2170

ANTONIO: Age must have one advantage, after all;
If, namely, it cannot escape from error,
It can control itself immediately.

You were at first concerned with reconciling
Me with your friend. Now I ask that of you.
Do what you can so this man finds himself
And everything is back again to normal.
I shall myself go to him just as soon
As I find out from you that he is calm,
And just as soon as you think that my presence   2180
Will not make matters worse. And yet, whatever
You do, do it within the hour. Alfonso
Is going back this evening yet, and I
Shall be accompanying him. Meanwhile, farewell.

[Exit.]

LEONORE *(alone):* This time, my friend, we are not in agreement.
My own advantage does not go along
Today with yours. Hence I shall use the time
In trying to win Tasso over. Quickly!   (2188)

ACT IV

A room.

TASSO *(alone):* Have you awakened from a dream, and has
   The fair illusion left you suddenly? 2190
   Did sleep subdue you on a day of highest
   Pleasure, and does it now hold and torment
   Your soul with heavy fetters? Yes, you wake
   And yet you dream. Where have the hours gone
   That played about your head with wreaths of flowers?
   Or those days when your spirit with free yearning
   Pierced through the blue that heaven spread afar?
   Yet you are still alive, you touch yourself,
   You touch yourself and are not sure you live.
   Is it my fault, is it another's fault 2200
   That I now find myself here as one guilty?
   Have I infringed a law, that I must suffer?
   Is not my entire fault a merit rather?
   I looked at him, and I was swept away
   By good will and the heart's deceitful hope
   That, bearing human features, he was human.
   Thus I went up to him with open arms
   And I encountered locks and bolts, no heart.
   O I had thought it out so cleverly
   How I was going to receive the man 2210
   Who this long time had seemed suspicious to me!
   But whatsoever has befallen you,
   Yet hold fast to one thing of certainty:
   I did see *her!* She stood right there before me!
   She spoke to me, and I did hear her speak!
   Her glance, her tone, and her words' lovely meaning,

67

Those are forever mine, time cannot rob me
Of them, nor destiny, nor yet wild fortune!
And if my spirit soared aloft too fast,
And if I all too swiftly gave vent to   2220
The flame within my bosom which devours
Me now, I still do not regret it, and
Though my life's fate were thereby lost forever,
I would devote myself to her and gladly
Go at her bidding though it called to ruin.
So be it! I still showed that I was worthy
Of that exquisite trust that gives me life,
That gives me life now at this very hour
That forcibly throws open the black portal
Of a long time of grief. — Yes, it is done!   2230
The sun of fairest favor sets for me
All of a sudden. Now the Prince averts
His gracious glance from me and leaves me here
To stand lost on a dismal, narrow path.
Those ugly winged things of double omen,
The loathly retinue of ancient Night,
They swarm forth now and whir about my head.
O where, O where shall I direct my step
To flee these noisome things that whiz about me,
And to escape from the abyss before me?   2240

[Enter Leonore.]

LEONORE: What has bechanced? Dear Tasso, did your zeal
And your suspicious thought so goad you on?
What happened? We are all in consternation.
Your gentle temper, your complaisant way,
Your rapid glance, and your just understanding
Whereby you give to each man what belongs
To him, your equanimity that bears
What noble men soon learn to bear but vain
Men seldom, wise control of tongue and lip —
Dear friend, I almost fail to recognize you!   2250
TASSO: And what if all those things had now been lost?

What if you came upon a friend whom you
Thought rich and found him suddenly a beggar?
You are quite right, I am myself no longer,
And yet I am such just as much as ever.
It seems to be a riddle, but is not.
The quiet moon that gives you joy by night
And with its shining lures your eye and spirit
Irresistably, it floats by day
An insignificant, pale, little cloudlet.   2260
I am outshone by splendor of the day.
You do not know me, I know myself no longer.

LEONORE: I do not understand what you are saying,
The way you put it, Friend. Explain yourself.
Did the gruff man's offense hurt you so deeply
That you completely fail to recognize
Yourself and us as well? Confide in me.

TASSO: I am not the offended one; you see
Me punished here because I gave offense.
The sword would cut the knot of many words   2270
Quite easily and fast, but I am captive.
You hardly know — do not, dear friend, be frightened —
But you now find your friend inside a jail.
The Prince is punishing me like a schoolboy.
I will not argue with him, cannot do so.

LEONORE: You seem to be upset more than is proper.

TASSO: Do you think me so weak, so much a child,
That such a fall could shatter me at once?
The thing that happened does not hurt me deeply;
What hurts me is the thing it signifies   2280
For me. Just let my enviers and foes
Alone to act. The field is free and open.

LEONORE: You entertain a false suspicion of
Many of them, I have convinced myself.
Nor does Antonio bear you such ill-will
As you imagine. And today's vexation —

TASSO: I set that quite aside, and only take

Antonio as he was and still remains.
His stiff-necked shrewdness always did annoy me,
His everlasting playing of the master.   2290
Instead of seeing if his hearer's mind
Is not already on the proper track,
He lectures you on things that you felt better
And more profoundly, does not hear a word
You say to him, and will misjudge you always.
To be misjudged, misjudged by a proud man
Who smilingly thinks he is so superior!
I am not old enough or wise enough
That I should merely smile back and endure it.
Sooner or later, it could not go on,   2300
We had to break; and later it would only
Have been just that much worse. I recognize
One master only, just the one who feeds me;
Him I will gladly follow, but no other.
I must be free in thinking and creating;
In action the world hems us in enough.

LEONORE: He often speaks of you with high esteem.

TASSO: Forbearingly, you mean, subtly and shrewdly.
And that is what annoys me, for he can
So smoothly speak, with such condition, that   2310
His praise becomes disparagement and nothing
Hurts you worse or more deeply than praise from
His mouth.

LEONORE: O if you only could have heard,
My friend, the way he used to speak of you
And of the talent gracious Nature gave you
Above so many. He unquestionably
Feels what you are and have, and he esteems it.

TASSO: A selfish spirit, O believe me, cannot
Escape the torments of its narrow envy.
A man like that may well forgive another   2320
His fortune, rank, and honor, for he thinks:
That you yourself will have if you so wish,

And persevere, and Fortune favors you.
But what has been alone conferred by Nature,
What lies beyond the reach of all exertion,
Forever unattainable by effort,
What neither gold, nor sword, nor shrewdness, nor
Persistence can achieve, that he will not
Forgive. He grant me that? He, who with stiff
Mind fancies he will force the Muses' favor?   2330
Who, when he strings the thoughts of many poets
Together, seems to see himself a poet?
He will far sooner grant my Prince's favor,
Which he would like to limit to himself,
Than that high talent which those Heavenly Ones
Have given to the poor and orphaned youth.

LEONORE: O if you saw as clearly as I see it!
    You are mistaken, he is not that way.

TASSO: If I mistake him, I mistake him gladly!
    I see him as my most insidious foe   2340
    And would be desolated if I had
    To see him as more lenient. It is foolish
    To be fair-minded all the time; that is
    Destruction of oneself. Are human beings
    So fair of mind toward us? O no! O no!
    The human being in his narrow nature
    Requires the double feeling, love and hate.
    Does he not need the night as well as day
    And sleep as well as waking? No, I must
    From now on look upon this man as object   2350
    Of my profoundest hatred; nothing can
    Deprive me of the pleasure of imagining
    Him worse and worse.

LEONORE: If you, dear friend, will not
    Desist from this opinion, I can hardly
    See how you can remain here at this court.
    You know what weight he carries, and must carry.

TASSO: How totally superfluous I have

Been here this long time, I well know, fair friend.
LEONORE: That you are not, that you can never be!
    You know how glad the Prince is, and how glad   2360
    The Princess is to live with you; and when
    The sister from Urbino comes, she comes
    Almost as much for your sake as her brother's
    And sister's sake. They all alike think well
    Of you, and each has total trust in you.
TASSO: O Leonore, what kind of trust is that?
    When has he ever said a word to me,
    A serious word, about his state? If ever
    There was a special case where, even in
    My presence he consulted with his sister   2370
    Or others, he did not ask my opinion.
    Always it was: "Antonio will be coming!
    We must write to Antonio! Ask Antonio!"
LEONORE: Instead of thanking him, you are complaining.
    If he is pleased to give you total freedom,
    He pays you honor, as he can pay honor.
TASSO: He lets me be, because he thinks me useless.
LEONORE: You are not useless just because inactive.
    Care and vexation you have held so long,
    Like a beloved infant, at your bosom.   2380
    I have considered often, and consider
    It as I will, — upon this splendid ground
    Where Fortune seemed to have transplanted you,
    You do not thrive. O Tasso! — Shall I say it?
    Shall I advise you? — You should go away.
TASSO: O do not spare the patient, dear physician!
    Give him the remedy, do not consider
    If it is bitter. — If he can recover,
    That is the thing to ponder, wise, good friend!
    I see it all myself, it is all over!   2390
    Him I can well forgive, me he can not.
    They need him, and, alas, do not need me.
    And he is shrewd, and I, alas, am not.

And he works to my harm, and I can not,
I do not like to harm him back. My friends,
They let it pass, they see it otherwise,
They barely make resistance, and should fight.
You think that I should leave. I think so too —
So then, farewell. I will endure that also.
You parted with me — may the strength and courage   2400
Be granted me to part with you as well.
LEONORE: O, from a distance everything looks purer
Which from near-by we find bewildering merely.
Then you will realize perhaps what love
Surrounded you on every side, what value
The loyalty of true friends has, and how
The wide world does not take the place of close ones.
TASSO: That we shall see. From childhood I have known
The world, the way it leaves one destitute
And lonely quite without concern, and goes   2410
Its way like sun and moon and other gods.
LEONORE: If you heed me, my friend, you never shall
Go through this sad experience again.
If you take my advice, you will go first
To Florence, and a friend will there most kindly
Look after you. Be of good cheer. That friend
Is I myself. I go to meet my husband
There in the next few days, and I can give
No greater joy to him or to myself
Than if I bring you with me to our midst.   2420
I shall not say a word, you know yourself
To what kind of a Prince you will be coming,
What kind of men that lovely city holds
Within its bosom, and what kind of women.
You do not speak? Consider well! Decide.
TASSO: It is delightful, what you say, so wholly
In keeping with the wish I entertain.
Only, it is too new. I beg you, let
Me think it over. I will soon decide.

LEONORE: I go away now with the fairest hopes   2430
    For you and us and also for this house.
    Consider, and if you consider rightly,
    You hardly can conceive a better plan.
TASSO: Just one more thing, beloved friend! Tell me,
    How is the Princess now disposed toward me?
    Was she annoyed with me? What did she say? —
    She did blame me severely? Speak quite freely.
LEONORE: Since she knows you, she easily excused you.
TASSO: Have I lost in her eyes? Don't flatter me.
LEONORE: Women's favor is not so lightly lost.   2440
TASSO: Will she release me gladly if I go?
LEONORE: If it is for your welfare, certainly.
TASSO: Will I not lose the Prince's favor too?
LEONORE: In his magnanimity you can rest safely.
TASSO: And will we leave the Princess all alone?
    You go away; though I meant little to her,
    I still know that I did mean something to her.
LEONORE: A distant friend provides us very friendly
    Association, if we know him happy.
    This will succeed, and I see you made happy,   2450
    For you will not leave here unsatisfied.
    The Prince so ordered, and Antonio
    Will come to see you. He himself now blames
    The bitterness within him which so hurt you.
    Receive him calmly when he comes, I beg you.
TASSO: In every sense I can stand up to him.
LEONORE: And Heaven grant me still before you go,
    Dear friend, to open up your eyes and show you
    That no one in the entire fatherland
    Hates, persecutes, or works you secret harm.   2460
    You surely err, and as you formerly
    Wove verse for others' joy, so now, alas,
    In this case you have woven an odd web
    To harm yourself. I shall do everything
    To rip it all asunder, so that you

May walk the fair pathway of life in freedom.
Farewell. I shall hope for a good word soon.
                    [Exit.]
TASSO *(alone):* I am to recognize that no one hates me,
    That no one persecutes me, that all cunning
    And all the secret webs were solely spun   2470
    And woven of themselves inside my head!
    I'm to confess that I am in the wrong,
    That I to many do injustice, who
    Have not deserved it of me! And this in
    An hour when my full right lies clear before
    The countenance of the sun, as does their craft.
    I am to feel profoundly how the Prince
    Grants me his favor with an open heart,
    Apportions gifts to me in bounteous measure.
    Just at the moment when he, weak enough,   2480
    Lets his eye by my enemies be darkened
    And surely lets his hands be fettered too!
    That he is being deceived, he cannot see,
    And that they are deceivers, I can't show him;
    So that he may be quietly deceived,
    So that they may deceive him comfortably,
    I am to bide in silence, even yield!
    And who gives me this counsel? Who so shrewdly
    Urges me with true and fond opinion?
    Lenore herself, Lenore Sanvitale,   2490
    My tender friend! Aha! I know you now!
    O why did I put trust in her lips ever?
    She was not honest, though she showed me ever
    So much her favor or her tenderness
    With her beguiling words! O no, she was
    And still remains a crafty heart; she turns
    Toward favor with a soft and clever tread.
    How often I have willingly deceived
    Myself about her too! Yet basically
    My vanity alone deceived me. Good!   2500

I knew her, yet kept flattering myself;
She is this way with others, I would say,
But with you it is frank and true opinion.
And now I see it, see it all too late.
I then was favored, and she clung so softly
To one who had been favored. Now I fall,
She turns her back on me, as Fortune does.
She comes now as a cat's-paw of my foe,
She glides up to me here and with smooth tongue
The little serpent hisses magic tones.   2510
She seemed so lovely! Lovelier than ever!
What healing was in her lips' every word!
Yet flattery could not conceal for long
Her false intention from me. The opposite
Appeared too clearly written on her brow
Of everything she said. I quickly feel it
When someone seeks the pathway to my heart
And does not mean it from the heart. I am
To leave? For Florence, as soon as I can?
And why for Florence? I see that quite well.   2520
There rules the new house of the Medici,
Not, to be sure, in open enmity with
Ferrara, but still silent envy with
A cold hand holds the noblest souls apart.
If I receive distinguished tokens of
Their favor from those noble princes there,
As certainly I might expect to do,
The hangers-on would soon make my devotion
And gratitude suspicious; they would succeed.
Yes, I will leave, but not the way you wish.   2530
Yes, I will go, and further than you think.
What is there for me here? Who holds me back?
O every word I understood too well
That I enticed from Leonore's lips!
From word to word I barely caught it, now
I know the whole of what the Princess thinks —

Yes, yes, that too is true, do not despair!
"She will release me gladly if I go,
If it is for my welfare." O! I wish
She had a passion in her heart that would   2540
Destroy me and my welfare! Far more welcome
Would be the death that seized me, than this hand
That coldly, stiffly, lets me go — I go! —
Be on your guard now and let no appearance
Of friendship or goodwill deceive you. No one
Deceives you unless you deceive yourself.

[Enter Antonio.]

ANTONIO: I come to have a word with you here, Tasso,
    If you can and desire to hear me calmly.
TASSO: Action, you know, is still forbidden me.
    It well befits me to wait and to listen.   2550
ANTONIO: I find you tranquil, as I wish to do,
    And gladly speak to you from my free heart.
    First I dissolve, and in the Prince's name,
    The tenuous bond that seemed to hold you captive.
TASSO: Caprice now sets me free, as once it bound me.
    This I accept and do not ask for trial.
ANTONIO: Then let me say to you: It seems that I,
    By words, have hurt you deeply and still worse
    Than I myself, stirred up with many passions,
    Had realized. No word of insult dropped,   2560
    However, indiscreetly from my lips.
    As nobleman you've nothing to avenge,
    And as a man you won't refuse forgiveness.
TASSO: Which thing would hit the harder, hurt or insult,
    I will not now inquire. The former pierces
    The inner marrow, the latter cuts the skin.
    The dart of insult turns back on the man
    Who meant to wound; a sword well wielded will
    Soon satisfy opinions of all others —
    But an offended heart recovers slowly.   2570
ANTONIO: Now it is my turn to say urgently

To you: Do not draw back, fulfill my wish,
And the wish of the Prince who sends me to you.
TASSO: I know my duty, and I will give in.
    As far as possible, all is forgiven.
    The poets tell a story of a spear
    That could by friendly application cure
    A wound which it had once itself inflicted.
    The tongues of human beings have that power;
    I shall not hatefully resist it now.   2580
ANTONIO: I thank you, and I wish that you would put
    Me, and my will to serve you, to the test
    Immediately with confidence. Tell me,
    How can I help you? I will gladly do so.
TASSO: You offer just what I myself was wishing.
    You brought me back my liberty again;
    Now get for me, I beg, the use of it.
ANTONIO: What can you mean? Explain that in plain terms.
TASSO: You know that I have finished up my poem.
    It still lacks much of being truly finished.   2590
    Today I did present it to the Prince,
    But hoped to ask a favor as I did so.
    To make request of him at the same time.
    A number of my friends I find assembled
    Just now in Rome; some have expressed already
    In letters to me their opinions of
    Some passages; I have been able to
    Use much, but many things seem to require
    Yet further study; several passages
    I should not like to change unless they can
    Convince me more than has been done so far.   2600
    All that can not be done through written letters,
    Their presence would resolve the problems quickly.
    I meant to ask the Prince myself today,
    But found no chance. Now I dare not attempt it
    And can hope for this leave through you alone.
ANTONIO: It does seem ill-advised for you to leave

Just at the moment when your finished work
Commends you to the Prince and to the Princess.
A day of favor is a day of harvest,
One must be busy as soon as it ripens.   2610
And if you go away you will gain nothing
And maybe lose what you have gained already.
A mighty goddess is the present moment.
Learn to perceive her influence: stay here.

TASSO: There's nothing that I need to *fear*. Alfonso
Is noble, he has always shown himself
Magnanimous to me. And what I *hope* for,
I want to thank his heart for, not obtain
A grace by stealth; nor will I take from him
What he could then regret once having given.   2620

ANTONIO: Then do not ask him to release you now.
He will do so reluctantly, and I
Fear almost he will not do it at all.

TASSO: He will be glad to, if correctly asked,
And you can do that as soon as you wish.

ANTONIO: But tell me, what grounds am I to allege?

TASSO: Just let my poem speak from every stanza!
What I intended merits praise, far though
My goal may have outdistanced my achievement.
There was no lack of industry and effort.   2630
The cheerful course of many lovely days,
The quiet spaces of so many nights,
Were all devoted to that holy poem.
I modestly had hopes of coming close
To those great masters of the ancient time,
Of boldly calling our contemporaries
Out of long sleep to noble feats, and then
Perhaps of sharing fame and peril of
A holy war with noble Christian armies.
And if my poem is to wake the best   2640
Of men, it must be worthy of the best.
What I have finished I owe to Alfonso;

Now I should like to owe him full completion.

ANTONIO: That very Prince is here, as well as others,
Who can guide you as well as Romans can.
Complete your poem *here,* here is the place,
Then go to Rome to put it into action.

TASSO: Alfonso first inspired me, and will be
The last one surely to give me instruction;
Advice from you and from the clever men   2650
Whom our court has assembled, I prize highly.
You shall decide in case my friends in Rome
Fall short of totally persuading me.
But I must see them all the same. Gonzaga
Has formed a court for me, to which I must
Present myself, and I can hardly wait.
Flaminio de' Nobili, Angelio
Da Barga, Antoniano, and Speron Speroni!
You surely know these men. — What names those are!
With confidence and with concern alike   2660
They fill my mind, which gladly bows before them.

ANTONIO: You think of yourself only, not the Prince.
I tell you he will not release you now;
And if he does, it will be with reluctance,
You surely will not ask what he will not
Grant willingly. Must I be intercessor
For something I myself can not approve?

TASSO: Will you refuse me the first service when
I put your proffered friendship to the test?

ANTONIO: True friendship is shown by refusal at   2670
The proper time, and often love confers
A harmful gift by thinking more about
The asker's wishes than about his welfare.
You seem to me at just this present moment
To think good what you eagerly desire,
And to demand right now what you most want.
An erring man makes up by vehemence
For what he lacks in truth and strength of forces.

My duty bids me moderate as far
As possible the haste that sends you wrong.   2680
TASSO: I long have been familiar with this tyranny
   Of friendship, which of all the tyrannies
   Seems most intolerable to me. You think
   A different way, and fancy therefore
   You have the right opinion. I concede
   That you desire my welfare; only do not
   Ask me to look for it along your path.
ANTONIO: Am I to do you harm right at the start,
   Cold-bloodedly, with full clear consciousness?
TASSO: I will deliver you from that concern!   2690
   You will not hold me from it by these words.
   You did pronounce me free, and this door which
   Leads to the Prince stands open for me now.
   I leave the choice to you. You, or else I!
   The Prince is leaving. This is not the moment
   For tarrying. Choose quickly. If you do
   Not go, I'll go myself, come what come may.
ANTONIO: Let me obtain a brief postponement only
   From you, and wait until the Prince returns.
   Just not today!
TASSO: No, no! This very hour   2700
   If possible! My feet are burning on
   This marble pavement here; my mind can not
   Find rest until the open roadway dust
   Is swirling all around me in my haste.
   I beg you! You can see how awkward I
   Would stand in speaking with my master at
   This moment; you see — How can I conceal it? —
   That at this moment I can not command
   Myself; no power in this world can do
   So either. Chains alone could hold me back!   2710
   Alfonso is no tyrant, he pronounces
   Me free. How gladly I obeyed him once!
   Today I cannot so obey. Just for today

Leave me in freedom so my mind can find
Itself. I will return to duty quickly.
ANTONIO: You make me dubious. What shall I do?
I clearly see that error is contagious.
TASSO: If I am to believe you wish me well,
Get what I want as far as you are able.
The Prince will then release me, and I will   2720
Not lose his favor, will not lose his help.
That I will owe to you, and I will thank you.
But if you hold an old grudge in your heart,
If you prefer me banished from this court,
If you want to destroy my fate forever
And drive me helpless into the wide world,
Then stick to your opinion and oppose me!
ANTONIO: Because I am to harm you anyway,
I will, O Tasso, choose the way you choose.
The outcome will decide who was in error!   2730
You want to go away! Then I predict:
You scarcely will have turned your back upon
This house when your heart will long to be back,
And stubbornness will drive you on. Dejection,
Perplexity, and grief in Rome await you.
And you will fail your purpose there as here.
I say this now no longer to advise you.
I am foretelling only what will happen,
And I invite you now beforehand to
Confide in me when worst has come to worst.   2740
I shall speak to the Prince now, as you ask.
                    [Exit.]
TASSO *(alone):* Go on, and go with the conviction that
You have persuaded me to what you will.
I'm learning to dissimulate, for you
Are a past master, and I catch on quickly.
Life forces us to seem, in fact to be,
Like those whom we had boldly, proudly, once
Despised. I now perceive quite plainly all

The artfulness of this fine court intrigue!
Antonio wants to drive me out of here   2750
Without its seeming that he drives me out.
He plays the wise one, the considerate one,
Just so I may be found inept and sick,
Appoints himself my guardian to debase
Me to the level of a child, whom he
Could not force as a lackey. Thus he clouds
The Prince's brow, the vision of the Princess.
He thinks that they should keep me: Nature did
Endow me after all with some fine talent,
But then again unfortunately accompanied   2760
The lofty gift with many weaknesses,
With pride unbounded, with exaggerated
Sensitivity and gloomy mind.
There's nothing for it; destiny so formed
This one particular man this way, so people
Must take him just the way he is, endure him,
Put up with him, and some fine day, maybe,
Enjoy from him, as unexpected gain,
Some things or other which can give them pleasure.
But as for other matters, he must be   2770
Allowed to live and die as he was born.
Do I still see Alfonso's steadfast mind?
Defying foes and stoutly shielding friends,
Do I see him as he confronts me now?
Oh yes, I now see fully my disaster!
It is my fate that everyone will change
Toward me alone, but toward all others will
Stand firm and true and sure, will lightly change
At just a breath, and in a moment's time.
Did not this man's arrival of itself   2780
Destroy my fate completely in one hour?
Did it not overthrow the structure of
My happiness from its most firm foundation?
O must I live to see this yet today?

Yes, just as everyone once thronged to me,
So everyone deserts me now; as each
One sought to draw me to himself and hold me,
So they all cast me off now and avoid me.
And why is that? Does he alone outweigh
The weight of my worth in the scales and all   2790
The love that I once had in such abundance?
Yes, everyone flees from me now. You too,
Beloved Princess, you withdraw from me!
She has not in these dismal hours sent
A single token of her favor to me.
Have I deserved that of her? — You poor heart,
For whom it was so natural to adore her! —
When I but heard her voice, how my breast was
Shot through with inexpressible emotion!
When I beheld her, day's bright light was dimmed   2800
For me; past all resistance her eye would,
Her lips would, draw me on, my knees would hardly
Support me, and I needed all
My strength of mind in order to stand upright
And not fall down before her feet; I hardly
Was able to dispel that ecstasy.
Hold fast, my heart! And you, clear mind of mine,
Be not here overclouded! Yes, she too!
Do I dare say it? I scarcely believe it;
I do believe it and want to suppress it.   2810
She too! She too! Excuse her fully, but
Do not conceal it from yourself: she too!
O these words, which I ought to doubt as long
As any breath of faith still lives within me,
Yes, these words, they engrave themselves like one
Of Fate's decrees on the bronze tablet-margin
Of the full-written tables of my torment.
Now only are my enemies made strong,
Now I am robbed forever of my strength.
How can I fight if *she* is in the army   2820

Opposed? How can I bide in patience if
She does not from afar lend me her hand?
If *her* glance does not meet the suppliant?
You did make bold to think it, did express it,
And it is true, before you could be frightened.
And now before despair with claws of bronze
Rips up your senses, tears them all asunder,
Accuse the bitter destiny, repeat
And then repeat again: She too! She too!   (2829)

ACT V

A garden.
Alfonso. Antonio.

ANTONIO: At your behest I went a second time   2830
  To Tasso, and I have just come from him.
  I spoke to him, I pressed him urgently,
  But he will not give up his point of view
  And ardently pleads with you to release him
  So he may go to Rome for a brief time.
ALFONSO: I am annoyed, I will admit to you,
  And I would rather tell you that I am
  Than hide it and make the annoyance greater.
  He wants to leave, then. Good! I will not keep him.
  He wants to go away, to Rome. So be it!   2840
  Just so as Scipio Gonzaga does
  Not get him from me, that shrewd Medici!
  That is what has made Italy so great,
  Each neighbor vying with all others to
  Possess the better men and make use of them.
  A Prince who does not gather talents round him
  In my eyes is a General without
  An army, and whoever does not hear
  The voice of poetry is a barbarian,
  Whoever he may be. I found this one   2850
  And chose him; I am proud to have him serve me,
  And since I have done so much for him thus far,
  I should not like to lose him without cause.
ANTONIO: I am embarrassed, for I bear the blame
  Before you for what happened here today.
  I too am willing to admit my error;

86

It now is for your favor to forgive.
But if you could imagine that I have
Not done the utmost to conciliate him,
I would be inconsolable. O speak   2860
To me with gracious mien so that I once
Again may get control and trust myself.
ALFONSO: Antonio, no, on that score be assured.
By no means do I put the blame on you.
With this man's mind I am too well acquainted,
I only too well know what I have done,
How often I indulged him, how much I
Forgot that it was actually for me
To give him orders. Man can make himself
Master of many things; necessity   2870
And length of time will hardly bend his mind.
ANTONIO: When others do a great deal for one man,
It is but fitting that the one in turn
Should diligently ask himself what helps
The others. One who has so trained his mind,
Who has ransacked all sciences and all
The knowledge that it is vouchsafed to us
To know, should he not be obliged twice-over
To rule himself? And does he think of that?
ALFONSO: It seems we're not supposed to be at rest!   2880
As soon as we plan to enjoy ourselves,
A foe is given us to test our valor,
A friend is given us to test our patience.
ANTONIO: Man's first and foremost duty, choosing food
And drink, since Nature has not bounded him
So straitly as the beasts, does he fulfill it?
Does he not rather let himself be lured
Like children by what gratifies his palate?
When does he mingle water with his wine?
Sweet things and spices and strong drink, one after   2890
The other he consumes with eager speed
And then complains about his turbid mind,

His fiery blood, his all too vehement being,
And puts the blame on Nature and on Fate.
How bitterly and foolishly I often
Have seen him argue with his doctor, comic
Almost, if anything is comic that
 Torments a man and plagues his fellow creatures.
"I have this trouble," he says plaintively
And much chagrined: "Why do you vaunt your skill?   2900
Make me get well!" — "All right!" replies the doctor,
"Then don't eat this and this." — "I can't do that." —
"Then take this medicine." — "Oh no; It tastes
So vile, my nature just revolts at it." —
"Well, then, drink water." — "Water? That I won't!
I am as water-shy as rabid people."
"Well, then, there is no help for you." — "Why not?"
"Your trouble will go on and gather trouble,
And if it doesn't kill you, it will bother
You more and more with every day." — "Fine! What   2910
Are you a doctor for? You know my trouble,
And you should know the remedies as well,
And make them palatable, so that I need
Not suffer to get rid of suffering."
You smile yourself, but is it not the truth
That you have heard him say this very thing?
ALFONSO: I've heard it often and excused it often.
ANTONIO: It is most sure that an intemperate life
    Just as it gives us wild, oppressive dreams,
    Will in the end make us dream in broad daylight.   2920
    What else is his suspicion but a dream?
    Step where he may, he thinks he is surrounded
    By enemies. No one can see his talent
    But that he envies him, and none can envy
    But that he hates and fiercely persecutes him.
    Thus he has often burdened you with his
    Complaints: forced locks and intercepted letters,
    Poison and daggers! What all won't he fancy?

You had these things investigated, did so yourself;
Did you find anything? Hardly the semblance.   2930
No Prince's patronage will make him safe,
No friend's devotion can assuage his feelings,
And will you promise peace and happiness
To such a man, and look for joy from *him?*

ALFONSO: You would be right, Antonio, if I looked
    To find in him my own direct advantage.
    But it is my advantage that I do
    Not look for direct and immediate profit.
    Not all things serve us in the selfsame way.
    He who needs much must use each thing in its   2940
    Own fashion; thereby he will be well served.
    That is the lesson that the Medici
    Have taught us, that the Popes themselves have shown.
    With what consideration, with what princely
    Patience and forebearance those men have
    Borne many a great talent which seemed not
    To need their wealthy favor, yet did need it!

ANTONIO: Who is not well aware of it, my Prince?
    Life's pains alone teach us to prize life's goods.
    While still so young he has attained too much   2950
    For him to savor it contentedly.
    O if he were obliged to work and earn
    What now is offered him with open hands,
    He would exert his powers manfully
    And would from step to step be satisfied.
    But a poor nobleman already has
    Attained the goal of his best wishes when
    A noble Prince selects him for his court
    Associate and with a generous hand
    Removes him from all want. If he gives him   2960
    His confidence and favor too, and seeks
    To raise him over others, to his side,
    Be it in war, in business, or in talk,
    Then I should think the modest man might honor

His happiness by silent gratitude.
And Tasso has, on top of all of this,
A young man's finest happiness: his country
Has recognized him and has hopes for him.
Believe me, his capricious discontent
Rests on broad cushions of his lucky fortunes.   2970
He comes; release him graciously, and give
Him time in Rome, in Naples, or wherever
He will, to look for what he has missed here,
And what he can find only here again.

ALFONSO: Does he want to go back first to Ferrara?

ANTONIO: He wants to stay on here in Belriguardo.
The most important things that he needs for
His trip he will have sent him by a friend.

ALFONSO: I am content. My sister will go back
Directly with her friend, and I on horseback   2980
Will still reach home before them. You will follow
As soon as you have tended to his needs.
Give orders to the castellan for what
He needs so he can stay here at the castle
As long as he may wish and till his friends
Have sent his luggage to him, and till we
Send him the letters which I am quite willing
To write to Rome. But here he comes. Farewell.

[Exit Antonio. Enter Tasso.]

TASSO *(with reserve):* The favor which you have so often shown me
Appears to me today in its full light.   2990
You have forgiven what I thoughtlessly
And insolently committed in your presence.
My adversary you have reconciled,
You will permit me to absent myself
From your side for a time, and you are willing
Magnanimously to keep your favor toward me.
I now depart in total confidence,
And hope that this brief respite will cure me
Of everything that now oppresses me.

My spirit shall uplift itself anew, 3000
And on the path that I first trod with joy
And vigor, cheered and heartened by your glance,
Shall once again be worthy of your favor.

ALFONSO: I wish you happiness upon your journey
And hope you will come back to us entirely
Cured and in cheerful mind. Well satisfied,
You then will bring us back twofold reward
For every hour you have deprived us of.
I shall write letters for you to my people
And friends of mine in Rome, and I much wish 3010
That you will everywhere keep in close touch
And have full confidence in them, as I
Consider you, though absent, as my own.

TASSO: You overwhelm, O Prince, with favor one
Who feels himself unworthy and can not
So much as thank you at the present moment.
Instead of thanks I make a plea to you!
My poem lies most closely at my heart.
I have done much, and have spared neither effort
Nor diligence upon it, but too much 3020
Of it is wanting still. So I should like
To put myself to school once more down where
The spirit of great men still hovers round,
And hovers with effect. My song would then
More worthily rejoice in your approval.
O give those pages back to me which I
Now know with shame to be in your possession.

ALFONSO: You will not take away from me today
What you have hardly brought to me today.
Between you and between your poem let 3030
Me step as intercessor. Take care not
To injure by strict diligence the lovely
Naturalness that now lives in your rhymes,
And do not hear advice from every side!
The thousandfold ideas of as many

Different men, who contradict each other
In life and in opinions, these the poet
Will wisely take as one and not shrink from
Displeasing many so that he may that
Much better please so many others. Yet   3040
I do not say that here and there you should
Not modestly make some use of the file.
I herewith promise you that in short time
You will receive a copy of your poem.
From your hand it will stay in my hands, so
That I, together with my sisters, may
First really have some pleasure in it. If
You bring it back more perfect, we shall then
Enjoy it with a higher pleasure and
In some points warn you only as a friend.   3050
TASSO: Embarrassed only, I repeat my plea:
Please let me quickly have the copy. My
Whole mind now dwells upon this work, and now
It must become the thing it can become.
ALFONSO: I quite approve the impulse that so moves you!
And yet, if it were possible, good Tasso,
You should enjoy the free world for a brief
Time and amuse yourself, improve your blood
By taking of a cure. Then you would find
The excellent harmony of senses thus   3060
Restored would give you what you now are seeking
In vain in all your gloomy zealousness.
TASSO: My Prince, it seems that way; yet I am healthy
When I can yield to my own industry,
And hence my industry will make me well.
You long have seen how I do not thrive in
Free luxury. Tranquillity gives me
The least tranquillity. This temperament
Of mine, I feel, alas, is not disposed
By Nature to drift down upon the days'   3070
Soft element to the broad seas of time.

ALFONSO: All that you think and do, leads you deep down
    Into yourself. On every side of us
    There lie abysses dug by destiny,
    The deepest being here within our hearts,
    And it gives us delight to plunge therein.
    I beg you, tear yourself away from *you*.
    The man will gain all that the poet loses.

TASSO: It is in vain that I repress that impulse
    Which surges day and night within my bosom.   3080
    When I can neither write nor meditate,
    Life is no longer life for me. Try to
    Forbid the silkworm to continue spinning
    Though it is spinning on to its own death.
    It will evolve its precious weft from deep
    Within its inner self and will not cease
    Till it has cased itself in its own coffin.
    O would that a good god would give us also
    The destiny of that same enviable worm,
    To spread our wings abroad with speed and joy   3090
    In a new valley of the sun!

ALFONSO: Hear me!
    You give a double pleasure of life to
    So many people; learn, I beg you,
    To know the value of the life that you
    Still have with ten-fold riches now. Farewell.
    The sooner you return to us, the more
    Superbly welcome to us you will be.
                    [Exit.]

TASSO *(alone):* So hold still firm, my heart, that was quite right!
    It is hard for you, it is the first time
    You can and choose thus to dissimulate.   3100
    You heard, that was not his true person speaking,
    Those were not his own words; it seemed to me
    An echo of Antonio's voice was sounding.
    O have a care! You will be hearing it
    From all sides from now on. Be firm, be firm!

It is a question of a moment yet.
One who learns late in life how to dissemble
Has the advantage of an honest look.
It will work if you only practice on them.

(after a pause)

You gloat too soon in triumph. There she comes.   3110
The gracious Princess comes! O what emotion!
She enters; in my bosom my vexation
And my suspicion are dissolved in sorrow.

[Enter the Princess.]

PRINCESS: You think of leaving us, or rather you
    Will stay behind in Belriguardo for
    A time yet, Tasso, then depart from us?
    I hope it will be for a short time only.
    You go to Rome?

TASSO: I will direct my way
    There first, and if my friends receive me kindly,
    The way I hope they will, then I perhaps   3120
    Will give the final touches to my poem
    With patience and great care while I am there.
    I will find many men assembled there
    Who well may be termed masters of all sorts.
    In that first city of the world does not
    Each spot, each stone, speak audibly to us?
    How many thousands of mute teachers beckon
    In solemn majesty and friendly-wise.
    If I do not complete my poem *there,*
    I never will complete it. But, alas,   3130
    I feel no luck attends on any project.
    Change it I will, but never finish it.
    I feel, I feel indeed that mighty art
    That nourishes us all, that strengthens and
    That quickens wholesome minds, will ruin me,
    It will drive me away. I hurry forth.
    I want to get to Naples.

PRINCESS: Do you dare?

The strict proscription has not yet been lifted
Which fell upon you and your father both.
TASSO: Well may you warn me, I have thought of that.   3140
    I will go in disguise. I will assume
    The poor coat of a pilgrim or a shepherd.
    I will slip through the city where the movement
    Of thousands easily conceals the one.
    And I will hurry to the shore and find
    A boat at once with willing, kindly people,
    With peasants, who have come from market and
    Are going home, with people of Sorrento.
    For I must hurry over to Sorrento.
    There lives my sister, who once used to be,   3150
    With me, my parents' joy amid their sorrow.
    I will be quiet in the boat and then
    Will step in silence on the land and softly
    Go up the path, and at the door will ask:
    "Where does Cornelia live? Would you please show me?
    Cornelia Sersale." Friendly-wise
    Some spinstress will point out the street for me
    And indicate the house. I will climb higher.
    The children will run after me and stare
    At my wild hair and at the gloomy stranger.   3160
    I will come to the threshold. Open stands
    The door, and I will step into the house —
PRINCESS: Look up, if that is possible, O Tasso,
    And recognize the danger you are in!
    I spare your feelings, or I would say to you:
    Is it quite noble to speak as you speak,
    Is it quite noble to think only of
    Yourself, as if you did not hurt friends' hearts?
    Is what my brother thinks concealed from you?
    Or how both of us sisters value you?   3170
    Have you not felt it and not recognized it?
    Has everything been changed in a few minutes?
    O Tasso, if you want to go away,

Do not leave grief and care behind for us.
                (Tasso turns away.)
How comforting it is, when some friend is
About to go away for a brief time,
To give him some small gift, if it is only
A new cloak or a weapon. But to you
One can give nothing more, because you throw
Away in anger everything you own.   3180
You choose the black smock and the pilgrim's wallet
And the long staff, and voluntarily
Go off in poverty and take from us
What you with us alone might well enjoy.
TASSO: Then you would not drive me away entirely?
O sweetest words, O fair and precious comfort!
O plead my cause! Take me in your protection! —
Leave me in Belriguardo here, transfer
Me to Consandoli, or where you will!
The Prince is owner of so many castles,   3190
So many gardens that are tended all
Year long, in which you hardly walk *one* day,
Perhaps no more than for a single hour.
Yes, choose the most remote of them which you
Will not be visiting for years on end
And which perhaps is lying now untended,
And send me there! And there let me be yours!
How I will take care of your trees, and cover over
The lemon trees with boards and bricks in autumn
And see them well protected with bound rushes.   3200
The lovely flowers in the flowerbeds
Will strike broad root, and every spot and pathway
Shall be kept clean in perfect tidiness.
And let me take care of the palace too!
I'll open windows at the proper times
So dampness will not damage the fine paintings;
The walls so beautifully adorned with stuccoing,
I'll clean them with a gentle feather-duster,

The pavement floor will shine with spotlessness,
Not one stone, not one brick shall be displaced,   3210
No grass shall grow out of a single crack.
PRINCESS: I find no remedy within my heart
　　And find no solace for you or — for us.
　　My eye looks round to see if some god might
　　Not send us help, might not reveal to me
　　A healing herb, a potion of some kind,
　　That would bring your mind peace, and peace to us!
　　The truest word that flows forth from my lips,
　　The best of curatives no longer works.
　　I have to leave you, and yet my heart can   3220
　　Not give you up.
TASSO:　　　　　　Is she the one, ye gods,
　　Who speaks now with you and takes pity on you!
　　And could you fail to know this noble heart?
　　And in her presence was it possible
　　Faint-heartedness once seized and overwhelmed you?
　　No, it is *you*, and I too now am I!
　　O go on speaking and from your lips let
　　Me hear all comfort! O do not withdraw
　　Your counsel from me! Speak: What shall I do?
　　So that your brother can forgive me, so   3230
　　That you yourself might be glad to forgive me,
　　So that you all might count me once again
　　With joy among your own? O tell me that!
PRINCESS: It is but little that we ask of you.
　　And yet it seems to be too much by far.
　　You should entrust yourself to us as friend.
　　We shall ask nothing from you which you are
　　Not when you are contented with yourself.
　　When you yourself are pleased, you give us pleasure,
　　You only sadden us when you avoid it.   3240
　　And though you do sometimes make us impatient,
　　It is that we would like to help you and
　　Unfortunately we see there is no help

If you yourself will not seize the friend's hand
Which, yearningly extended, does not reach you.
TASSO: It is your very self, the way you met
Me like a holy angel that first time.
Forgive the mortal man's dull vision if he
At certain moments failed to recognize you.
He knows you now again! His soul is opened   3250
Fully, adoring none but you forever.
My heart is wholly filled with tenderness —
She, she stands before me. What emotion!
Can it be aberration draws me to you?
Or madness? Is it heightened sense, which can
Alone seize on the highest, purest truth?
Yes, it is the emotion which alone
Upon this earth can give me happiness,
And which alone made me so miserable
When I resisted it and tried to banish   3260
It from my heart. I meant to fight against
This passion, and I fought and fought with my
Profoundest being, impiously destroyed
My very self, which you belonged to wholly —
PRINCESS: If I, O Tasso, am to hear you further,
Then moderate this heat, which frightens me.
TASSO: But will a goblet's brim retain the wine
That foams and runs and boils and overflows?
With every word you lift my happiness,
With every word your eye more brightly shines.   3270
I feel myself in inmost soul transformed,
I feel myself disburdened of all pain,
Free as a god, and owe it all to you!
The power ineffable that masters me
Streams from your lips. Yes, you make me entirely
Your own, and nothing of my total self
Henceforward will belong to me again.
My eye grows dim with light and happiness,
My senses fail, my foot no longer bears me.

You draw me to you irresistibly   3280
And my heart surges toward you without check.
You have completely won me, and forever,
So take my entire being unto you!
> *(He falls into her arms and presses
> her to him.)*

PRINCESS *(thrusting him aside and hurrying away):*
Away from me!

LEONORE *(who has been visible for a time in the background,
hurrying up):* What happened? Tasso! Tasso!
> *(She follows the Princess.)*

TASSO *(on the point of going after them):*
My God!

ALFONSO *(who for a time has been seen approaching with
Antonio):* He's lost his senses! Hold him fast!
> *(Exit.)*

ANTONIO: O if, as you are always thinking that
You are surrounded by your foes, some foe
Were standing by you now, how he would gloat!
Unhappy man, I hardly find my breath!
When something wholly unexpected happens,   3290
When our gaze chances on some monstrous thing,
Our mind stands stock still for a time, for we
Have nothing which we can compare to it.

TASSO *(after a long pause):*
Fulfill your office, I see it is you!
Yes, you deserve the princely confidence.
Fulfill your office and proceed to torture
Me slowly, now the staff is broken for me,
To death. Go on and draw, draw out the arrow
So I may fiercely feel the barbed hook
That tears my flesh!   3300
You are the tyrant's precious instrument;
Be prison keeper, be the torturer,
How well, how fittingly both things become you!
> *(toward offstage)*

Yes, go, then, tyrant! You could not dissemble
Until the very last, gloat in your triumph!
You have the slave now well in chains, you have
Him saved aside for torments well thought out.
Go on, I hate you! And I fully feel
The loathing that the upper hand occasions
That pounces impiously and with injustice.   3310

(after a pause)

At last I see myself now banished here,
Driven away and banished like a beggar.
They crowned me to be led up to the altar
Adorned like any sacrificial victim!
And they enticed from me on this last day
My sole possession in this world, my poem,
With smooth words got it for themselves and kept it!
In your hands is my sole possession which
Could have commended me in any place
And which alone could save me from starvation!   3320
I clearly see why I should take vacation.
It is a plot, and you are leader of it.
So that my poem does not get perfected,
So my name may not spread abroad still further,
So enviers may find a thousand flaws,
So I at last may be forgotten wholly,
That's why I should get used to idleness,
That's why I should indulge myself, my senses.
O worthy friendship, precious thoughtfulness!
I thought that the conspiracy was loathsome   3330
Which was spun round me restless and unseen,
But it has now become more loathsome still.
And you, you Siren, who so tenderly,
Celestially enticed me, now I see
You suddenly! But why, O God, so late!
But we so willingly deceive ourselves
And honor reprobates who honor us.
No, human beings do not know each other;

Only galley slaves know one another
Who pant for breath chained to a single bench;   3340
Where none has anything to ask and none
Has anything to lose, they know each other;
Where each man frankly says he is a scoundrel
And takes his fellow-men for scoundrels too.
But we politely mistake other people
So that they will mistake us in their turn.
How long your sacred image hid from me
The courtesan who plays her little tricks.
The mask now falls, and I behold Armida
With all charms stripped away. — Yes, that is you!   3350
Foreknowingly my poem sang of you!
And then the wily little mediatrix!
How deep degraded I see her before me!
I hear her rustle of light footsteps now,
I know the circle now round which she stole.
I know you all! Let that suffice for me!
If misery has robbed me of everything,
I praise it still; it teaches me the truth.

ANTONIO: I hear you, Tasso, with astonishment,
    Much as I know how lightly your rash mind   3360
    Pitches from one extreme point to the other.
    Reflect a bit, and overcome this rage.
    You blaspheme, you permit yourself word after
    Word which can be forgiven in your grief
    But which you never can forgive yourself.

TASSO: O do not talk to me with gentle lips,
    From you I want to hear no words of wisdom!
    Let me have this dull happiness, so as
    Not to reflect, and then to lose my mind.
    I feel my very inmost bones all mangled   3370
    And I am still alive to feel the pain.
    Despair in all its fury seizes me
    And in the hellish torment that consumes me
    Blaspheming is a tiny sound of pain.

I want to go away! If you are honest,
Then show it, and let me get out of here!
ANTONIO: I will not leave you in this great distress.
And if your self-control fails you entirely,
My patience certainly shall not fail me.
TASSO: Then I must give up to you as a captive?   3380
I do give myself up, and so it's over.
I offer no resistance, that is best —
Then let me painfully repeat once more
How beautiful it was, what I have squandered.
They're going away — O God, I see the dust
Already rising from their carriage wheels —
Foreriders out ahead — There they go, there
They disappear! Did I not come from there?
Now they are gone, and they are angry with me.
O if I could but kiss his hand once more!   3390
O if I could but say farewell again!
Could only once again say: "O forgive me!"
And hear him saying: "Go, you are forgiven!"
But that I do not hear, will never hear —
O I will go! Let me just say farewell,
Just say farewell! But give, O give me back
The present time for just a moment yet!
Perhaps I will get well again. No, no,
I am cast out, am banished, I have banished
Myself, and I will never hear that voice   3400
Again, and I will never meet that glance
Again, No, never —
ANTONIO: Let a man's voice remind you who is standing
Beside you here, not without being touched:
You are not quite so wretched as you think.
Be strong! You give in too much to yourself.
TASSO: And am I then as wretched as I seem?
Am I as weak as I appear before you?
Has everything been lost? Has sorrow not,
As if the earth had quaked, transformed the building   3410

Into a gruesome heap of shattered rubble?
Is there no talent left now to divert
Me thousandfold and to support me?
Is all the strength extinguished which once stirred
Within my heart? Have I become a nothing,
An utter nothing?
No, everything is here, and I am nothing!
I have been stolen from myself, and she
From me!

ANTONIO: Though you seem utterly distraught,
    Compose yourself. See yourself as you are!   3420

TASSO: Yes, you remind me at the proper time! —
    Will no example out of history
    Avail? No noble man come to my sight
    Who suffered more than I have ever suffered,
    So by comparison I may be steadied?
    No, all is lost! — One thing alone remains:
    The gift of tears is given us by Nature,
    The cry of anguish, when at last a man
    Can bear no more — To me above all else —
    She left me melody and speech in grief   3430
    To cry out all my plenitude of anguish,
    And if men in their torment must be mute,
    A god gave me the power to tell my pain.

               (Antonio steps up to him and takes
                   him by the hand.)

O noble man! You stand secure and silent,
I only seem to be a storm-tossed wave.
Reflect, however; do not gloat in triumph
For all your power! Mighty Nature, who
Gave this rock firm foundation, also has
Conferred mobility upon the wave.
She sends her storm, and then the wave is driven   3440
And rolls and swells and, foaming, overturns.
Upon that wave the sun was mirrored once
So beautifully, and constellations rested

Upon that bosom, which then gently swayed.
The splendor now has vanished, peace has fled. —
I know myself no longer in my peril
And am ashamed no longer to confess it.
The helm is shattered and the ship is cracking
On every side. With an exploding noise
The ground is riven underneath my feet!   3450
I now throw both my arms around you. Thus
The helmsman at the very last clings to
The rock on which he was about to founder.   (3453)

TORQUATO TASSO

is startlingly modern in its content.
In this play of 1790 Goethe presents
five admirable friends—three men
and two women—who bear each other
all good will, who speak at length together amid the leisure of a rural
vacation, and who close their fine
spring day by beholding the total
ruin of the youngest and most tal-
ented member of their group, the
Renaissance poet Torquato Tasso,
who later won fame for his "Jerusalem Delivered."

None of the friends intended ill,
none of them lied, but somehow the
faulty aspect of each one's character
was exposed in fateful juxtaposition.
Through long association they have
somehow consistently misunderstood
each other; still more, the four realistic ones have misunderstood the sensitive poet; most of all, the sensitive
poet has misunderstood them. He first
thought of them as demigods, but he
ends by taking them for demons, both
views being equally far from the
truth. If Tasso is himself much to
blame for his own disaster, he also
suffers more desperately than the
others.

The general failure of communication between human beings is
Goethe's secondary theme. The primary theme which leads to it is the
particular failure of communication

continued on back flap